B   Heidenreich, Steve   20
HEIDEN   Running back
REICH

13C1313

DATE			
FEB 1 3 1985			

RUNNING BACK

Introduction

The words, whispered, but firm and vibrant, were an admonition.

"Steve . . .

"Steve . . . !

"Stephen Alan Heidenreich, are you listening to me?"

Across the table, tucked away in a silent nook of the Indiana University library, a figure stirred. From behind an opened history book emerged the handsome profile of a young man that radiated strength and singlemindedness. Beth Burnside, waiting impatiently, watched as he slowly relinquished the book and his face finally appeared.

First, the tawny mustache. Then the eyes—dark, hooded, piercing. Finally, the smile. She loved it when he smiled. His was the smile of a man who was at peace with himself.

"It's almost eleven o'clock," she said. "We've got to go."

He nodded. "Did you know," he said, smugly, "that I'll probably ace this course. You expected that, I'm sure."

Beth's answer was to wrinkle her nose.

"What do you think you are, God?" she asked teasingly.

He laughed.

"No. Just a saint."

Quickly, he rose. As he pushed his chair back from the table there was a screeching that echoed in the hushed room. Heads began swiveling in their direction. The glares were stony.

Steve Heidenreich flushed with embarrassment. He could feel himself growing crimson. He was a private person, very intense and very sensitive, and he felt as if the glares were drilling holes through him. Nevertheless, he met the gazes, smiled, and shrugged.

They stepped from the warmth of the library into the icy March

1

night air. Beth pulled her coat snugly up around her neck while Steve unlocked the safety chain on his bicycle.

The walk from the library to the Kappa Kappa Gamma house, Beth's sorority, on East Third, was not far. The two dawdled, moving at a deliberately slow pace while Steve pushed his bicycle along beside him on the sidewalk. Their feet crunched in the new snow which had, that morning, whitened the streets and the rooftops of Bloomington. It was a quiet, unexpected snow, catching, as it did, the trees budding.

In the few months that Beth and Steve had known each other they had become inseparable. She had learned to read him perfectly and she could sense that on this night his mood was one of expansive exuberance.

Not so for Beth. She felt fidgety and ill at ease and she could not understand the feeling. Her breath crested and she shivered in the cold night frosted with stars. They talked quietly for a while. Suddenly he turned to her, a wide grin on his face.

"The qualifying number for today is . . ."

Beth caught his mood perfectly. "Let me guess . . ."

"I'll give you a hint. The number is more than two but less than four."

Beth smiled. "I've got it. It's three and you're one of them."

The subject of their guessing game was the 1976 United States Olympic Trials at which the American track and field team to represent the country at the Games in Montreal would be determined. Heidenreich was among the early qualifiers and, precisely 101 days from tonight, he would be running in one of the preliminary heats of the 1,500-meter event in Eugene, Oregon.

Steve Heidenreich was an extraordinary athlete. Eight months earlier, on July 4, appropriately, he had worn the colors of America in an international meet at Kiev, Russia. Three days after that he had finished third at Prague, Czechoslovakia, in the 1,500 with a time of 3 minutes 38.8 seconds, his lifetime best. The event was the metric mile, the time equivalent to that of a 3:56.0 mile. By adding seventeen seconds to the 1,500-meter time, one determines the mile time. Heidenreich's 3:38.8 was the seventeenth fastest 1,500-meter time in the world in 1975 and he was among the four fastest Americans in the event.

The publication *Track & Field News,* acknowledged authority in the sport, had ranked him number six in the United States in the 1,500 for the year 1975. It was a ranking based not on time alone but on consistency and performance in many major meets.

Beth looked at Steve as they approached the Kappa Kappa Gamma house. She began, tentatively:

"Look, I know it's getting late and we still have some work to do on this term paper. Wouldn't you like to go down to Nick's for a glass of wine? Or maybe we could check the Time Out and see who's there."

Silence.

". . . Well?"

Beth was feeling guilty because Steve had walked her home while he had so much farther to go to his apartment, and it was cold out. But she really did not want him to leave. The words were out of her mouth before she could think.

"Why don't you just not run tonight?"

Heidenreich's eyes locked with Beth's in a note of panic. She looked away, feeling as though she had just betrayed him. The look he gave her was more chilling than the raw March wind that whipped about them both. She might just as well have asked him to reach up and touch the moon. Impossible.

"I have to run. If I don't someone else will," he said.

Beth had never doubted that Steve would reach the summit he was aiming for. But at this moment, maybe for the first time, she realized his indomitable qualities and the deep well of resolve from which he drew.

She wrote in her journal of the incident later that night:

> It was as if all the great milers were his daily competitors. He may have been setting the pace at IU but the great runners all over the world were setting *his* pace. Maybe that's what makes a person great—keeping in mind his competitors rather than himself.

Steve hurried off, calling over his shoulder that he would phone her. He wheeled his bicycle to the apartment steps. Inside in the hall he found a note that his coach, Sam Bell, had wanted to speak to him.

On Woodbluff Court, a cul-de-sac in the midst of new homes on the east edge of Bloomington, Bell and his wife, Fran, were preparing for bed.

Bell had spent a good portion of the evening packing for a trip the next day that would take his Indiana University team to the University of Alabama at Tuscaloosa and later to the University of Florida at Gainesville.

It was not uncommon for college track and field teams from the northern states to migrate south for ten or fifteen days of training and competition in the sun, where muscles could be stretched and tested with a minimal fear of injury. It was not quite spring in southern Indiana. The ice had broken on the Jordan, a small brook that flows through the IU campus, but the weather was still more wintry than most athletes liked for intensive work-outs.

Bell flipped the channel on the television set in the bedroom to the news. Taking precedence over all but the most significant world, national, and local stories was the mounting excitement of the NCAA basketball tournament.

Basketball in Indiana is not a sport, it is a frenzied passion that permeates everyone's life in Hoosierland from December through March. In testament, cream-and-crimson toilet seats with the Indiana University insignia were beginning to appear in some of the most fashionable restrooms in Bloomington.

Hysteria. It mattered little to the noisy, skittish students swilling beer at Nick's English Hut that Gerald Ford, the incumbent, and Ronald Reagan were squaring off in the Illinois presidential primary, an electoral prize worthy of the nation's scrutiny. The only important thing was that two days later undefeated Indiana would play Alabama in the NCAA Mideast Regional at Baton Rouge, Louisiana. The IU track team's impending trip received cursory attention during the sports segment of the news. At 11:30, Bell switched off the set and went to bed.

Heidenreich looked at the phone message from his coach and then bounded up the stairs to his room to change into his running clothes. At the kitchen table Mark Schlundt, a discus thrower on the Indiana team and one of Heidenreich's roommates, was typing a report for a business course that was due the next day. Heidenreich hurried down the stairs, glancing at Schlundt as he went out the door. Outside, he put on mittens and pulled a stocking cap over his ears. Slowly he jogged past a line of cars parked on the apartment lot and to the entrance of Kinser Pike, a residential street that he ran often. He turned north.

Always, Heidenreich ran twice a day and one of his workouts was at night. It was a custom he had followed from the time he had been a junior in high school. Heidenreich's linear, fragile build matched perfectly that of what most people envision a distance runner to be. He was five feet ten inches tall and weighed 130 pounds. Lean and sinewy, he had long, slim legs and thighs not a great deal larger than his calves. His hips were narrow.

As he strode he held his arms about waist-high and his hands were cupped but not clenched. His feet struck the asphalt rhythmically, first at the ball of his foot, gently, and then rolling forward until he pushed off the toe. In the stilled silence there was only the sound of his even breathing and the impact of his shoes on the street.

On this night he ran at a pace between 5½ and 6 minutes for a mile. The snow underfoot, hardly a trace by now, would not be a problem, he thought. He picked up the pace a little, pleased that he felt so fresh but anxious to complete the five-mile loop and return to the apartment so that he could resume studying. He was sharing the work on a term paper with Beth. When he left her he promised that he would call her at 2:30 A.M. and report his progress.

Beginning a climb on a short incline Heidenreich was running close to the curb and judging his pace by watching a telephone pole that moved closer and closer. The first thing he heard was the sound of a motor . . . roaring as if it was leaping crazily ahead. Then he was aware of the glare of lights . . . headlights that seemed to be swirling all about him. Instinctively, he wanted to dive somewhere—get far from the traffic. There was nowhere to go. He was about to jump off the road and onto a snowy lawn but it was too late. There was the thud of metal colliding with human flesh.

Approximately ten minutes after Heidenreich had taken his first steps on Kinser Pike, Randy Hehr, a music student at the university, turned his red Datsun pickup truck south onto the same street.

A balky, sputtering cold engine forced Hehr to advance slowly. As the vehicle began to gain speed and reached the top of the small incline the headlights focused on a form that Hehr thought might be a body.

He braked the truck, stopping as close as he dared. He was horrified. It was, indeed, a body. Hehr, his heart tripping, sat nailed to his seat. He hoped that it was a staggering, indigent drunk who had fallen and, surely, would get up.

But if it wasn't, if whoever it was had been injured and needed immediate assistance, what could he do? Should he even get involved?

The irrational moment passed. Hehr's eyes caught sight of headlights coming from the opposite direction and he flashed his lights frantically.

"Aren't they trying to signal us?" asked Joe Berger, a passenger in the other car who noticed the flashing.

Chuck Lupton, the driver, nodded. He stopped and backed up as Hehr rolled down his window.

"Would you get out with me so we can see what is going on?" Hehr pleaded. The three walked together toward the body.

Berger and Lupton, consultants for a health and hospital planning firm, were in Bloomington on business. For Berger, a medic in Viet Nam, the scene suddenly yanked him back in time. He had a flashback of rice paddies, of shrapnel-torn limbs, of blood. One look at the body lying on its side and Berger knew that the young man was badly hurt. There was blood on the curb, on the street and on the red nylon hooded rain jacket. What none of the three could see was that the young man's head had been smashed and that there was an ugly, gaping wound on the right side of his skull from which the blood was spilling.

Lupton broke the silence. "What should we do for him?"

"Don't move him," said Berger, who took the car keys from Lupton and sped to a nearby Ramada Inn, confronting a sleepy night clerk and yelling: "Don't ask any questions; please, there isn't much time. Call the police and get an ambulance out here on this street. There's a man who is critically injured."

Meantime, Hehr had driven a short distance to his girlfriend's apartment and returned with a blanket. Lupton listened carefully to the victim's tremulous breathing. Soon the sound, ragged at first, became more regular. The young man stopped gasping and began a rocking motion, his body moving out into the street. He was whimpering.

It was when Hehr placed the blanket over the young man that he saw the tremendous amount of blood on his head, some of it already coagulating. Hehr thought that he probably had been beaten and dumped from a moving car.

Todd McCormick, a Bloomington policeman on patrol, was cruising in front of a Howard Johnson's motel on North Walnut when the radio in his squad car crackled.

"A 1050 PI (personal injury) accident on Kinser Pike south of the Highway 46 bypass," reported the police department dispatcher, who had registered the call from the Ramada Inn clerk. "An ambulance is on the way."

McCormick answered the dispatcher on his car radio. "Got it," he said. "I'm on my way."

McCormick made a U-turn, took a shortcut and was at the site within moments. He was used to seeing physical injuries, but he gasped when he saw the victim's broken skull. His training told him that the young man was gravely hurt.

"I thought he was going to die," McCormick said to a friend later that night. "I handled it as a fatality. I called for all cars in the north end of town to assist and I sealed off the street four blocks each way."

Two squad cars, the ambulance and a rescue van arrived quickly, filling the night with sirens. Moments later the ambulance left for Bloomington Hospital with the injured young man.

Richard Rak, a young neurosurgeon who had joined the hospital's staff only five and a half months earlier, was asleep at home when the call came from the emergency room.

"Doctor, we have a head patient. A young male . . . probably a university student. He appears to have been running and I think he was hit by a car."

Moments after Dr. Rak hung up, another number was dialed by one of the nurses on duty in the emergency room. It was 12:30 when the telephone jangled in the bedroom of the Bell home, awakening the coach from a fitful sleep. He fumbled for the receiver.

". . . Bloomington Hospital calling, Coach Bell. One of your runners has been hit by a car. He's about, oh, five-seven or five-eight and he has kind of brownish blond hair and a mustache. We found an IU trip schedule in a back pocket of the navy blue running sweatpants he was wearing. Can you come and identify him, coach?"

Panic engulfed Bell. The images of all of his athletes that resembled the description by the caller flashed through his mind.

Bell reached for the phone and dialed Mark Schlundt.

"Hello."

"Mark, this is Coach Bell. Do you know where Steve Heidenreich is?"

"Sure, coach. He's upstairs."

"Mark, the hospital just called me and said one of our runners has been hit by a car. I think it might be Steve."

"Wait a second. I'll check."

Schlundt ran up the stairs and knocked on Heidenreich's bedroom door. When there was no answer, he pushed the door open. Heidenreich's bed was untouched. Schlundt returned quickly to the phone.

"He's gone, coach. I heard him come in but I didn't hear him leave."

"That's all I wanted to know. I'm going to the hospital."

Sam Bell felt hollow as he dressed hurriedly. He opened the car door and climbed in, not wanting to believe what might be the truth. By the time his car had reached the corner, though, he was almost positive it was Heidi.

The coach drove into the hospital's parking lot and, pushing back drowsiness, scurried to the emergency room. Shoving the door open he entered and introduced himself to a nurse. He followed her to a small examining room off to one side and gaped in astonishment at what he saw. Every fear he had had was confirmed. Heidi was moaning and, although unconscious, he was thrashing and waving his arms and kicking strongly. Two nurses were telling him, "Hold still . . . hold still."

The coach heard a voice behind him. He turned and looked up into the eyes of a very tall man in a doctor's green gown who resembled a pink-cheeked choirboy. He shyly brushed back thick, unruly hair that had fallen over his forehead into his eye. Sticking out his hand he said:

"Hello, I'm Doctor Rak."

Bell grabbed him by the elbow. "How is he, Doctor?"

Rak showed Bell an X ray, tracing with his finger a jagged fracture that had split the skull open, starting at the top of Heidi's head and running adjacent to his ear and to the right side of his lower jaw, which was broken. The left side of the lower jaw also was shattered.

Bell was enraged at first. He felt helpless, as if someone had taken a sledgehammer to his gut.

"Stephen is in a coma," said Dr. Rak. "Do you know where he lives and where his parents are?"

Numbly, Bell nodded. He went to the nearest phone and asked the hospital operator to get him the number of Merle Heidenreich in Watertown, South Dakota.

When the phone rang at 1:15 A.M., Steve's father sat suddenly upright in bed, staring into the blackness. Time seemed to be suspended. He made his way to the living room, thinking that it might be Steve.

"He always was a great one for that," Merle recalled later. "All of a sudden he'd decide to call and it would be a quarter after eleven and he'd wake me up and I'd say, 'Do you know what time it is?' He would say, 'No, what time is it?' And I'd answer,

'It's eleven-fifteen and I've been sleeping!' "

". . . Oh."

Merle heard a phlegmatic voice tell him that it was Blooming-ton Hospital calling. With a sense of foreboding, he listened.

"Merle?"

"Yes . . ."

"This is Sam Bell, Merle. There has been an accident. Steve has been hurt badly. I want you to talk to Doctor Rak. He's a neuro-surgeon here in Bloomington. I'm at the hospital now."

Merle sat down on the sofa. He was aware that his hand holding the receiver was trembling. He heard some dialogue in the background and then another voice said, "Mr. Heidenreich . . . your son has been hit by a car." It was Dr. Rak.

"How bad is it?"

"Well, I think you should come. He has a skull fracture and his lower jaw is broken in two places. I need your permission for a cerebral angiography."

"Of course."

DeLoris Heidenreich, sensing the urgency in her husband's voice, was soon at his side.

"What . . . who is it?" she asked.

Merle Heidenreich placed a hand over the receiver and whis-pered . . . "It's Steve. He's been hit by a car."

"Oh, my God," exclaimed DeLoris. She slumped onto a stool by the sofa, her face pallid. She wanted to say some-thing, anything, but could not. She closed her eyes and si-lently prayed.

Immediately, they did the angiography, an X ray of blood vessels after the injection of a radio-opaque substance to show the out-lines of the veins. It disclosed a probable large blood clot on the right side of Steve's head.

Dr. Rak knew he would have to operate, and called Water-town again for permission. He explained to the parents what the angiography had shown.

"You should make plans to come here right away," said Dr. Rak with a deadly finality.

DeLoris Heidenreich interrupted. "Is . . . he," she asked, tugging at her husband's pajama sleeve.

"What?"

"Is he alive?"

"Yes," he answered softly as Dr. Rak continued to talk.

"We cannot leave Watertown until late morning and it will be afternoon before we can get there," Merle told the doctor.

"I see. Well, I will call you when I am finished with the surgery."

Merle placed the receiver on the cradle and, transfixed by his thoughts, stared distraughtly at the floor.

At 3:00 A.M., Beth Burnside's phone at the Kappa Kappa Gamma house still was silent. She was disturbed; piqued that Steve had not called—but also gripped by a sense that something was wrong. Somehow, she had a mental picture of what had occurred. As she pulled the bedcovers up around her chin she asked herself, "What if Steve was in an accident or something?"

At the hospital Dr. Rak was preparing for surgery. He worked silently and quickly, saying little, as was his nature when he was under pressure.

Steve Heidenreich was wheeled into the operating room. Dr. Rak grasped Heidi's right hand. "Help me," pleaded Steve Heidenreich, almost inaudibly. "Please . . . help me."

Then he glided, once again, into the deep vortex of unconsciousness.

1

As a runner, Steve Heidenreich showed promise even in eighth grade as a scrappy 100-pounder whose hair continually flopped over his eyes and whose glasses seemed constantly to be slipping to the edge of his nose. True, his body was bony and in the awkward process of maturation, and those feet of his, growing faster than the rest of his body, seemed to plod too long in the same place. But he demonstrated one necessary ingredient: strength of mind. If ever there was a sport that he seemed fitted for, it was running.

In the autumn of 1968 Heidenreich and Drake Titze were the only freshmen on the Watertown High School cross-country team and both had run in the state meet. It was to be the start of brilliant prep careers for the two and a rivalry that onlookers watched with more than usual interest as it burgeoned. In 1968 Steve was striding in the shadows of Titze, who had clocked times in the spring of that year which were excellent for one of his age. He ran a 4:31.4 mile and a 2:01 half-mile. Heidenreich was an 11-minute two-miler and a 5:10 miler.

Heidenreich was too small and weak to be a factor in most races, but his confidence and his willpower were bigger than he was. The demand for excellence that he placed upon himself was there. Frequently he would approach his track coach, Vic Godfrey, and tell him after races that he was the better runner and that he should have won.

"Fine," Godfrey would reply. "Start letting your legs do the talking. I'm tired of hearing what you should have done . . ."

Godfrey noted at year's end that Titze was the better of the two. Although Heidenreich seemed to be put together with equal parts of grit and guts, it was difficult to think of him as a future star. But how could Godfrey have known then of the unquenchable desire that was beginning to build inside Steve Heidenreich? Dwight Struckman, the Watertown varsity cross-country coach, saw the two runners differently than did Godfrey. Struckman judged that Heidenreich would eventually be superior, and he was right.

The city of Watertown stands on the flat, limitless farmlands of eastern South Dakota. It is prosperous, unhurried, quiet, one of the many middle-sized communities of America's Midwest that depend upon agriculture for a base of support and a means of livelihood. The family farm is the fiber that binds this section of the nation together. A beneficiary of the mighty glaciers that swept southward through neighboring Minnesota, Watertown is bounded on the west by Lake Kampeska and on the south by Lake Pelican.

The summer days rise certain here, with sunshine imprinted everywhere. Hard winters with crystal-clear air and, often, brutally cold temperatures are reflected in the faces of the stoic people who make Watertown their home. South Dakotans are a hardy lot; they have to be. The biting winds that blow heaps of snow across the frozen fields in the long winter months either toughen a man or strip clean his conviction and hasten his departure for points south.

Watertown is very much white, conservative Middle-America. Proud, Protestant, and squeamish if someone new should suddenly surface with ideas that would mean a radical shift away from center. In 1965 Watertown refused federal funds that could spur community development, preferring instead to do the job on its own. Then, in the early 1970s, this self-sufficient, pioneer posture gave way as Watertown saw the money it needed going to Huron, Mitchell and Sioux Falls, and the exigencies of harsh reality became apparent.

This, then, was the area which Merle and DeLoris Heidenreich chose to make their permanent home. Both had been raised near Aberdeen, South Dakota, and had met when they were students at Northern State College in Aberdeen. Merle Heidenreich, a visceral and resolute man, is earnestly spiritual. His roots go back to the farm, a farm twenty miles southwest of Aberdeen that had become home for his grandfather, Henry Charles Heidenreich, who had come to America as a stowaway from Blasheim, Germany. Merle will not inquire into someone else's thoughts unless invited to do so, and this reserved demeanor has been a trait that all know him by. He enjoys his achievements quietly as well. Merle, who teaches an American studies course at the high school, was once asked by a county Democratic committee to be a candidate for the South Dakota legislature. He declined, not wanting to take time from his family nor wanting to make the financial sacrifices necessary for the repeated trips to Pierre, the state capitol. In 1968 Bobby Kennedy had made a presidential primary campaign stop in Watertown. When Kennedy was assassinated one week later, Merle counseled his son, who had been unsettled by the death, on the meaning of life and the hereafter. "God is mysterious and His reasons are beyond our comprehension," said Merle. "It is as He wills. We accept them. The living go on silently, those of us who are left behind. We do not question. Bobby belongs now to God."

There were thirteen in the graduating class of Merle's high school. Baseball and basketball were the popular sports. When he was a senior, track and field was initiated—without a track to run on. "I have always been sorry that I didn't get a chance to run more than that in high school," says Merle, matter-of-factly. "Without even knowing what I was doing or with much of a training program of any kind I think I ran the 880 in 2:12, something like that, which wasn't too bad. It was fun and that was about it."

He did not run in college. "I tried it and it seemed I was always getting injured or I was getting sick," he recalls. "One spring I finally just gave up on it."

DeLoris Heidenreich's father, Erig Kinder, was a railroad man.

When DeLoris and Merle were attending Northern, she drove to classes. He lived in a basement apartment and walked, unless, as the wily Merle Heidenreich would explain to his children years later, when he needed a ride, "I'd know just how to time it when DeLoris Kinder was driving by."

Two weeks after DeLoris and Merle were married in 1952 they returned home from their honeymoon to find an Army induction notice in the mailbox. The Korean conflict had begun. Merle was sent to a base in the state of Washington, and then one day he was aboard a ship bound for Korea and saying goodbye to America, a full-fledged soldier. In Korea he was a member of an artillery battalion, stationed above the 38th Parallel but three miles in back of the front line. When he returned to America in 1953 his firstborn son, Steve, was waiting for him.

After Merle was discharged, he took a job teaching world history at Clark, a small community college near Watertown. He was also an assistant basketball coach, and was driving a bus to a junior high basketball tournament when his second child, Linda, was born in March 1955, at Aberdeen. One fall, he took on the job of coaching the girls' varsity cross-country team at the high school and wasn't paid a penny. He donated his time because he wanted to. "It wouldn't be Merle if he didn't," is how DeLoris once explained it, sighing deeply.

The next year the Heidenreich family moved into a cozy frame house at 320 South Broadway in Watertown. They have lived there since. A third child, Roger, was born in 1956. The last one, Laura, was born in 1962 and, happily for Merle, he was in attendance for both births.

DeLoris Heidenreich, a prim woman with gray hair, is family-oriented. "She is a born mother," says one of her close friends. "She doesn't wait on her family hand and foot—she has taught them to fend for themselves—but there isn't anything she wouldn't do. She is there when they need her, always ready to listen and help."

Frugality is a Heidenreich characteristic. Collecting material possessions is of no importance to DeLoris. In her moments of solitude she sews and reads and tends to her garden, often humming to herself in a light-hearted manner.

She works as a teacher's aide at an elementary school. Generally she does as much teaching as the teachers and plays piano for the students in the final fifteen minutes of each day. "Children identify with her," says Karen Kasperson, a woman with whom she worked closely. "She has an inner sense of understanding for all children . . . caring, a good listener, an arm around the shoulder, a hug. She is a mother to all the children in the room."

Always, the church has been the center of the Heidenreich family, succoring in times of need and distress. Merle has always seen to it that the children integrated the church into their daily lives. "School and coaching and his family and his church . . . I suppose that pretty well sums up Merle Heidenreich's life," says the Reverend Roger Fischer, pastor of the Lutheran church of which the Heidenreichs are members.

"He's very sure of himself and he is a humble person. He has a difficult job. When you try to be a teacher to the kids of the community it isn't easy sometimes. About seven or eight years ago two young men knocked on my door and said they had problems. They said they wanted to talk. I asked them:

" 'How did you happen to seek me out?'

"They said, 'Merle Heidenreich goes to your church, doesn't he?'

" 'Yes.'

" 'Well, we know him from school and we admire him.' "

Reverend Fischer continues:

"There is real closeness in the Heidenreich family, a caring among all of them. I think all of the kids are proud to be a part of the family because they found that security, that love, that interest which their mom and dad exhibited.

"Merle Heidenreich is unique in our church. He has been our superintendent of the Sunday School for twenty years. It's a tough job. You coax people to be teachers and you've got to be there every Sunday. You've got to be real faithful and, sure, take a little guff, too. It's a job that just plain takes a love for people. Merle has stuck at that and DeLoris has been his right-hand person. She doesn't have a title but she works as much as Merle does.

"He was elected chairman of the congregation. Normally, one does not give a person a second big job like that but I think the people wanted to because out of respect for him they just wanted to say, 'We appreciate you.' "

On a summer evening in Watertown, South Dakota, when shadows lengthened and the crickets chirped and the water out at Lake Kampeska was as smooth as glass, Steve would run past the house and hear DeLoris at the piano and Merle singing, selecting hymns for the Sunday service.

He would run on past on those summer evenings to some rural road near town. He believed, as his father did, that there was no shortcut to any goal. And Steve knew what he wanted early in life. His quest added to his reputation of one who seemed obsessed. Inwardly, a passion glowed.

In the autumn of 1968, Heidenreich's sophomore year, his friend Titze finished fourth in the state cross-country meet. Heidenreich was fourteenth. "Steve's presence was beginning to be felt," said Titze later. "For me it was nothing to worry about, but he was always there and always working."

Following the cross-country season Steve Heidenreich and Vic Godfrey entered the Tri-States Marathon. The 26-mile-385-yard race began at White Cloud, Kansas, looped through a tip of Missouri and ended at Falls City, Nebraska. Steve did no special training for the marathon. The many miles he had run during cross-country season had made his body hard and fit. However, after the marathon he was eleven pounds lighter than he had been when the crack of the starter's gun sent the mob of runners pushing forward.

"I weighed 101 when the race was over; I was nothing," says Heidenreich. "I was a toothpick and I had a fever. I was really dehydrated. They didn't give us water until we hit ten miles and twice again after that. It was a challenge, fun, something I wanted to do so that I could say I had done it.

"But it cost me three weeks of training. For three weeks after I could barely walk, much less run. I was in good shape until we got to twenty-two miles; Vic and I were running together. Then we came to a beast of a hill and I started to feel it. My legs hurt so bad and the sensation of pain in my calves was tremendous. I kept truckin' on but people were passing me—some of them would talk with me, keep encouraging me. We got into town and I knew I had only two miles to go and I said, 'Heck, you've got it made, buddy. You can crawl two miles.' I got to the track; we had to go once around it. I started my sprint but I didn't have any kick. There wasn't anything there. . . . Not a thing.''

Godfrey, who left Heidenreich after twenty-two miles, finished ten minutes ahead of his aching companion. Godfrey was tenth in 2:57.30. Steve Heidenreich, at age fifteen and in his first marathon, ran 3:07.29 and placed seventeenth.

In Heidenreich's spring track season his times improved greatly. He ran a 4:42 mile, a 10:23 two-mile and a 2:06 half. Titze progressed at an equal rate, clocking a 4:23.5 mile and a 1:56.6 half that smashed the state record.

Amid this, a new name had surfaced—that of Jeff Schemmel from Madison, a city south of Watertown. Schemmel, a gifted runner, was a freshman in 1969 and he ran a remarkable 4:23.6 mile and easily defeated Heidenreich. ''I looked at his running style and I thought it was super,'' says Schemmel. ''Even though I was running well, he had me worried.'' Clearly, the battle lines for the next two years were being drawn.

Yet, as outstanding as Titze's 1:56.6 and Schemmel's 4:23.6 were, they paled in comparison to a performance by a senior with white-hot ambition from Coos Bay, Oregon. His name was Steve Prefontaine and he ran an 8:41.6 two-mile, a national high school record then.

Some of Heidenreich's progress in 1968 surely could be traced to the fact that he began training twice a day. He got up at six o'clock each morning and jogged five blocks to Godfrey's house and out they would go for four miles. The winter that year was awful, no impetus to get anyone running. ''I dreaded hearing that knock on my door when the wind was howling outside and the snow was falling,'' says Godfrey. ''That boy, he seldom missed a day.''

Heidenreich wrestled through his sophomore year but then he

quit and became a runner only. Winter, spring, summer, autumn. He had not been a particularly good wrestler, but the workouts did make him stronger. There is a lot of similarity between wrestling and running. Both are individual sports, both require courage. One has to keep at them with dedication to make any progress. "I had to have one sport to compete in all the time during the year," says Heidenreich. "I love to compete and I had always wanted to be an athlete. In our high school at that time athletes had a lot of respect. I wanted to be in that group pretty bad."

As May of 1969 rolled into June Titze was the acknowledged leader. He felt uneasy, however, when he started to see the figure of Heidenreich over his shoulder. It unnerved him.

Few youngsters grow up knowing they will become runners. Not in America where professional athletes are deified and the sports of basketball, football and baseball are popularized. Why did Steve eliminate these others? Why track over, say, basketball? Why did he choose running?

"I had success," says Heidenreich. "It's as simple as that. I was a pretty frail kid. I had tried football and gotten my head beat in. I tried wrestling and it was OK. It was one-on-one competition; just you and the other guy. I liked individual sports."

Heidenreich's enthusiasm for running kept him going. "I didn't find it difficult. It took up some time but that was good because I didn't want to study. I needed something to use my time. If it wasn't for track it would have been something else, like maybe shooting pool, doing something ridiculous—getting into trouble. That's probably what it would have been."

As Heidenreich's infatuation increased, his adjustment to running became easier. And, typically, there was time devoted to being a teen-ager. He was not intent on following a narrow path that led him only to the locker room.

"After practice," he says, "I would goof around and have fun. I started the morning runs on the advice of Vic Godfrey. He said running twice a day would make me better. It did. Really, the only adjustment I had to make was in timing the day."

Godfrey left Watertown following Heidenreich's sophomore

year to become head cross-country coach at the University of Wisconsin-Parkside. Godfrey had convinced Steve during that summer before he entered the eleventh grade that he should attend the Olympia Sports Village at Upson, Wisconsin, a camp where a young runner could devote full time to his passion. There was seclusion at Olympia, with rustic, serene runs on soft paths, through dry mounds of leaves that crackled underfoot, through woods in the mist of the early mornings before a broiling sun burned away the dew.

When Heidi's stay at Olympia ended, Godfrey, who was on the camp's staff, drove him to Ironwood, Michigan, where he could board a bus for Watertown. "I was convinced then in talking with him that he was going to be one tough runner," says Godfrey, "although how tough I didn't even *begin* to appreciate."

2

When Heidi returned to Watertown in late August he began running with Drake Titze and the two would sometimes go off discovering a variety of routes to avoid boredom.

Since they ran at a pace which was far too swift and uncomfortable for others they usually went alone. But for them, it was a challenge and still beneficial. Training runs which cause constant physical distress play games with the mind. The runner quickly starts believing he is tired and talks himself into strength-sapping fatigue.

The lay of the land near Watertown, pool-table flat, provided a far different terrain in summer from that which the runners tackled in the autumn cross-country season. Racing over the hills and green sod, bobbing and sweeping into sharp turns marked with colored flags, bursting along corridors outlined with long white lines of lime or chalk, and rushing, exhausted, into the finish chute on wobbly legs can be a remarkable experience. Often vivifying. Often gratifying.

Comparing times for cross-country is futile. Courses can never be the same. Some are laid out on golf links. Some include a stretch on paved roads and then take the runners again into the woods. Kenny Moore, twice a marathoner on the United States Olympic team, says there is no experience as "pure" as cross-country. "Cross-country sensitizes the runner," he once wrote,

21

"not only to the country he crosses but to his own physiology.

"He becomes a connoisseur of tiredness, distinguishing, for example, the light-headed sensation of a five-mile jog following a series of sprints from the stiff, irritable fatigue near the end of a twenty-mile run. Patterns of frost and fog, the growth and withering of grass, induce an awareness of the land's rhythms. The nearness of one's own rhythms, of breath and heart and footfall, assures the runner his place. Such a run offers a chance for self-examination as well, a chance to discover one's sensitivity and to find out how one reacts to a face full of spider web in a dark glen."

Heidi welcomed the changeable surroundings that are not found in running on a track with its incessant repetition. Running the hills was not meaningless pain. Once he achieved fitness, the ordeal ebbed. One day he began to feel part of a very basic esthetic ritual—he was a man crossing the earth, unaided, as it presented itself to him. These were the rewards that the sport communicated to him.

The high school and college cross-country seasons in America are only two to three months in duration, and they require long, relaxed runs during the summer to build a base of endurance. Racing differs widely from that in Europe, where runners sometimes slog through mushy courses, leap ditches and hurdle barriers.

When a doughty group of runners reported to Watertown coach Dwight Struckman in the fall of 1969 for the cross-country season, the greatest distance-running era—high school or college—in the history of South Dakota was beginning.

Until then, the long winters had precluded extended training for prep distance runners, or so many coaches and school administrators thought. They were caught up in the erroneous assumption that year-round training would be injurious to a teenager's tender body. And training twice a day simply was not to be considered. At last, though, South Dakota joined a growing number of state high school associations across the country that were liberalizing training techniques for runners and, as a result, times began dropping dramatically.

Among South Dakota runners, miler Loren Kambestad of Bristol was the first to disprove the rigid, insular theories. He was followed by Watertown's skilled duo of Steve Heidenreich and Drake Titze, Madison's Jeff Schemmel, Jim Reinhart of Sioux Falls, Jim Trego of Winner and, later, Warren Eide of Watertown. The new training obviously paid off. Heidenreich eventually became a Big Ten Conference champion at Indiana University and Schemmel a Big Eight Conference champion at Kansas State University. Titze ran at the University of Missouri and Reinhart at Notre Dame.

Heidenreich had one necessary element to be a great runner: He had the will to endure. But he had something else as well. His future as a runner had been genetically fixed at birth when he was endowed with a higher percentage of slow-twitch muscle fibers than fast-twitch fibers, which contract more rapidly. The combination of slow-twitch and fast-twitch cells that a runner is born with determines whether he will be a sprinter or will be competent in the distances, since the secrets of speed and endurance reside in the fibers. The runner who has a greater percentage of fast-twitch cells would have difficulty becoming an accomplished distance runner. The runner with more slow-twitch fibers could probably never become a sprinter.

Other than the one marathon he ran, (and he had no desire to run another!) Heidenreich never competed in distances of more than two and a half miles in high school. At Indiana University he ran the mile and the half-mile because his coach knew he could gain points in those events. He might have been effective in longer events but why gamble? Thus his role in college was determined early and there were no deviations.

On their long, slow distance runs Heidi and Titze learned together how to become good runners. They practiced proper breathing, technique and form, and they checked each other.

Cross-country training is done on the roads or the golf course where mileage can be accumulated. Usually at the start of the season, and rarely thereafter, the runner will go to the track for a workout that can sharpen his speed. After that, it's long workouts for endurance. It was on one of their long runs that Titze had to stop, doubled over with a sharp pain that seemed to be centralized under his rib cage. It was a stitch, a spasm of the diaphragm muscle, and can usually be attributed to faulty breathing. This experience taught them not to breathe from the chest but with the belly, expanding it as they inhaled. This is a natural breathing pattern and can give the distance runner greater body efficiency, exactly what he is trying to achieve.

They ran for an hour at a stretch, concerning themselves not with speed but with piling up mile after mile. They skimmed along with no apparent effort, learning to conserve their strength and energy, sucking in gallons of oxygen as they went.

Running the hills taught them relaxation and put a spring into the stride and strength into the spirit. The stamina they sought was achieved naturally in the bodily process of an increase in the pressure of blood through the heart and capillaries for long periods daily during their runs. As the waste products (carbon dioxide, perspiration) were being removed more quickly and the blood flow was being enlarged they were able to go on and on for longer distances without feeling fatigued.

After the two had acquired a strong base of endurance in sustained, overdistance running, they increased the ability of their bodies to adapt to stress through all-out interval training on a track. They alternated fast and slow runs with an interval of rest between the fast runs. A typical workout was fifteen 110-yard dashes in fourteen seconds, each followed by a 330-yard jog; ten 220-yard dashes in thirty seconds, each followed by a 220-yard jog; and six 330-yard sprints in forty-five seconds, each followed by a 550-yard jog. These helped to establish a strong kick or sprint.

As Struckman, a small, slender man who himself had twice been a College Division All-America distance runner at South Dakota State in the early 1960s, watched his squad move through an easy workout on the soft turf of the municipal golf course, he paid close attention to Heidenreich and Titze. Their strides looked bouncy and fluid; and the coach was pleased. At the end of practice Heidenreich, his eyes sparkling, came to Struckman.

"Coach," said Heidenreich, firmly, "I think that this is going to be my year. I don't know exactly how I can tell that . . . it's just a special feeling, that's all."

Struckman smiled. "It's good that you feel that way, Steve. If you are willing to work, good things can come your way. Now I want you to cool down. Run an easy mile. No sprinting or surging. Feel that you are totally relaxed. Check your wrists and be sure they are loose. Keep your body fairly erect. Don't lean too far forward."

On their runs Heidi and Titze checked each other's posture. Ideally the runner should be erect from the face to the feet with no lean, and should use minimum arm action to conserve oxygen. Leaning forces the leg muscles to exert an upward force to counteract the lean which results in an awkward, choppy stride.

Heidi kept his stride short. He focused his eyes on a pole or a tree ahead of him as he ran, and if the object did not jiggle like a butterfly in flight he knew he was not overstriding.

In the proper positioning of his carriage, Heidi's shoulders, chest, and hips faced straight ahead with little side-to-side swiveling. If his legs felt heavy he swung his arms faster. The corresponding action made his legs move faster.

He concentrated on where his foot struck the ground. The point of contact should be directly under the knee, not out in front of it. And not being a sprinter he did not run up on his toes. Running this way over long distances puts too much pressure on the arch and can cause knotting in the muscles. When his foot landed flat he found it to be the most comfortable.

He experimented with his breathing, exhaling through his mouth and nose every second time his right foot struck the ground. Every so often he exhaled the "bad" air from his lungs with a brisk "whoosh!"

Heidi knew it was important to check his stride and balance and arm swing periodically. When his concentration lapsed and his mind wandered, he lost his sense of pace and defects began to creep into his form.

He made sure his shoulders were relaxed and his arms loose. This prevented his body from swaying as he ran. He never clenched his fists. If he did, the muscles in his arms and shoulders tightened and hindered a balanced, easy stride. Knee lift was another check point. The foot cannot go forward without knee lift and there can be no good knee lift if the hips are not facing forward and squared.

The season started with a four-mile road race. Titze defeated Steve by ten seconds. The gauntlet had been dropped.

On September 27, at Aberdeen in the Roe Granger meet, the breakthrough came for Steve Heidenreich. He vanquished Titze for the first time ever in a meet or a workout. Titze finished third in the race.

Heidi was rightfully proud but he celebrated silently, without lording it over his friend. His joy was ephemeral. Winning was such a special feeling that he vowed to himself he would let nothing stop him in his pursuit of the top rung on the ladder. And if he had to avoid others, go off by himself to get what he wanted, that's how it would be.

While Heidi's victory was a springboard, psychologically if for no other reason, Struckman was reluctant to look upon it later as the singular incident that made a real runner of Steve Heidenreich. "I don't remember seeing one special change after he had beaten Titze," says Struckman. "But I do know that winning was the paramount thing in his mind most of the time. I doubt that anyone could say they saw him deciding, 'Well, now I've accomplished this and here is my next goal.' "

On October 4 at the Watertown Invitational Heidenreich and Titze tied, holding hands as they crossed the finish line. The tie was the direct result of neither wanting to lose to the other's tactics in a small, unimportant race. In eight other races that season, Titze won on five occasions and Heidenreich three.

At the state meet, over a 2.2-mile course, Heidenreich placed second in 11:28. Titze was fourth in 11:34. Drake's respect for his teammate deepened. "I began to fear his ability," he said later. "Until then Steve was not much of a threat but he was working harder. Instead of losing confidence from the many times I beat him, he tried all the more to do better the next time out. It was easy to admire Steve. He had tremendous desire to achieve: Nothing steered him away from that. His confidence was sky-high, higher at first than it should have been considering his achievements. . . . He never gave up."

Heidenreich would simply not concede that anyone was better. Each loss represented to him the fact that others were further advanced, more ready, more fit. He'd just come back and try again. Early on, Steve developed a dislike—almost a hatred—for his opponents. If they beat him he swore revenge. He was becoming a loner, and some onlookers, who thought he had started to get callous, misconceived his shyness. His silent ferocity spilled over only in his races, however. He did not make excuses for his defeats, just resolved that he would do better.

Struckman agreed. "Steve had heart in a race, there's no doubt about that," he says. "I mean, if it was a case of losing or dying . . . He'd die first."

Now that the pattern had been broken and Heidenreich knew he no longer would always chase Titze's heels, Struckman could sense the pulse quickening. "Drake had relatively rich parents," says the coach. "He had so many things going. He was good in speech, he was good in music, whereas Steve basically had athletics. Period. Steve was more determined than Drake was.

"When I decided that there was more promise there for Steve than for Drake I based it mainly on practices, the energy that was being put forth and the degree of excitement that was shown toward upcoming meets. To Drake, they were more or less par for the course. To Steve, they were high points. He looked forward with anticipation to each one of them.

"They both saw them as challenges but to Steve there was more to it. He began to overtake Drake and became one of the great runners in the state. It was his way—his desire—to be somebody, I think. It was his way of accomplishing that."

As winter's winds stripped autumn's golds and browns from the trees, Steve Heidenreich had already decided what he wanted. He wanted to be the best. Desperately.

3

Steve Heidenreich, runner, was shaped in a manner similar to the greats who had come before him. Like Finland's fabulous Paavo Nurmi, who won six Olympic gold medals in his career, and like Czechoslovakia's Emil Zatopek who, in the 1952 Olympic Games at Helsinki, incredibly won the 5,000-meter, the 10,000-meter, and the marathon, an event he had never before run. Nonetheless, Zatopek destroyed the Olympic marathon record with a 2:23:03.2. By the time the runner-up had crossed the finish line, Zatopek was calmly eating an apple. "The marathon is a very boring race," he observed laconically.

Zatopek's and Nurmi's training philosophies strongly influenced Vic Michelson, the stocky, enthusiastic head track coach who replaced Vic Godfrey at Watertown in 1970. Michelson also subscribed to the theories of Arthur Lydiard, the New Zealand visionary whose principles of conditioning and phenomenal success with unknown runners had lifted him to a unique spot among the superb international coaches in the early 1960s.

Lydiard believed that hard work could make anyone—anywhere—run faster and farther. He learned by experimenting with different methods himself before asking his runners to try them.

Lydiard discovered that the first step to enjoying running was to achieve perfect fitness, a fitness that would enable a runner to confront great distances with ease at a steady speed.

"I felt inadequate with my collegiate instruction and with my past studies of running," says Michelson. "Of course, you can read anything but to put it to work is another thing. I hear too many adults today say, 'Here's how it should be done but I can't do it.' Double standards bug me. I hate 'em! So I thought, 'Well, I'll go through what these runners did, to find out what it's really like for myself.' "

Michelson found everything he could read on Nurmi and Zatopek. Of Nurmi, the Flying Finn, a barrel-chested, indefatigable runner who (legend has it) lived on a diet of black bread and dried fish, Michelson learned that he would carry a stopwatch in his right hand when he ran. Other runners looked back over their shoulders to see where the rest of the field was. Nurmi looked at his watch to see where *he* was. If he was where he thought he should be, he was satisfied. He used the watch to time himself as he passed fenceposts on his training runs. Afterward, Nurmi would take a steam bath and conclude his day with a roll in the snow.

Zatopek, his face contorted with anguish when he ran, his hand clutching his side, his shoulders hunched, had a style that was anathema to the purists. He twisted; he jerked; he strained.

Zatopek's training intrigued Michelson. Zatopek ran in the winter on a path in the woods, through mud, snow, and ice, in military boots when he was in the Czech army. At night he carried a flashlight when he ran.

Nurmi and Zatopek both inspired Michelson. "In the middle of the South Dakota winters I'd read a chapter in one of the books that described their styles," says the coach, "and I'd think, 'Man, if those guys can run in the snow and ice I can too, and I can train.' So I'd try it and I'd say, 'Well, now, I'm doing it and I'm not getting sick, so why can't the kids do it?'

"And the kids? They said, 'We'll do it!' and away we went . . ."

The lineage had been formed. Michelson was revolutionary in South Dakota. Few coaches could equal his zest or his progressive training techniques which tried to emulate as closely as possible the conditions of the two great runners he had studied.

"Eliminating the forests, which Watertown does not have,"

Michelson explains, "I thought we could reproduce other training factors that Nurmi and Zatopek had. We'd run the trestles of railroad tracks. We'd run through plowed fields—they can be chunky and difficult. East of Watertown we found hills with big rocks on them and you'd really have to apply steam to climb them.

"If we slipped and hurt ourselves a little, well, Nurmi and Zatopek did also. I figured if we were going to be any good when the spring rolled around we'd have to run in the winter and under difficult conditions. I don't think there's an excuse: There is always a place to run, even if it is in the snow. If the cars can get around, why can't we? Nurmi had been driven by an obsession to run and run well. I thought Steve was a little like him."

For the first time, Michelson stocked the high school library with books on running. He introduced the Watertown area to *Runner's World* magazine. "The kids would look at it and say, 'Well, hey, maybe we could be good enough to be in it someday.'"

With Godfrey gone, Heidenreich abandoned his early morning runs and began to run at night. Even in those savagely cold winters with temperatures that dipped to 30 below, he would put on a ski mask, a heavy sweatsuit, and mittens, and at ten o'clock he'd begin a five-mile run through the streets of Watertown. On the nights that were bitterly cold, his footfalls would produce a S-C-R-U-N-C-H! S-C-R-U-N-C-H! S-C-R-U-N-C-H! on the crystallized snow as he jogged, a solitary figure passing beneath the street lights.

"I ran at night because I found it hard to run in the morning and be at school by 8 A.M.," says Heidenreich. "Plus, I found at night I ran much faster and I was more relaxed. There were places to run. In South Dakota the snowplows do a good job of clearing the roads."

Winter turned into spring. Michelson, viewing his track and field team from afar, saw a double challenge.

"To learn what a guy is about—that is a key to coaching," says Michelson. "I learned a lot about Heidenreich. At first, he seemed like a quiet guy, looking through the bushes to see where he could go. And then the bush started to thin out and, maybe, it got thinner for me as well because soon we knew what we both wanted. I wanted him to be successful, as I do any kid, and he wanted success badly. He didn't have to beat everybody in the rest of the state; he had somebody in his own backyard he had to beat.''

That was Drake Titze, and if not Titze, there was Jeff Schemmel, who ripped off a 4:29.9 and beat Heidenreich (4:32.8) at the opening of the season. Michelson was not concerned with Schemmel at the moment, though. He decided to test them all and assemble a strong two-mile relay foursome that could run well. The Howard Wood Relays at Sioux Falls seemed a plausible place; it was a big meet. On the night before the meet, Michelson's phone rang at home.

It was Merle Heidenreich who introduced himself and explained quietly that Steve had tripped in a parking lot and that his knee, which had met the cement with a crash, was ballooning. What to do?

''Keep ice on it all night, and if you think he can run, bring him to the meet,'' Michelson told Merle. The next afternoon Steve sat in the back of the family station wagon with his leg outstretched during the drive to Sioux Falls.

Steve Heidenreich jogged lightly for an hour before the meet, testing his tender knee. He pronounced it okay. He took the baton for the third leg in the relay race and, with an excitement that was greater than his pain, he rocketed to a 1:55.3 split, and blew the race open. Titze anchored with a 1:56.2. Watertown's time of 7:55.1 was an all-time South Dakota record.

One week later, at the conference meet, it was Schemmel again in the mile. Running with absolute efficiency, he won with a 4:17. Heidenreich defeated Titze by the thickness of his singlet in 4:21. Heidenreich, however, did not lament the loss. As a matter of fact, he was happy. He could see himself getting good, very good, and he liked what he saw. ''My confidence was building and after a 4:21 I said, 'Hmmm. I know I can run 4:16; I know I can run at least that fast.' ''

Michelson, searching for a way to help his young athletes

break through the pain barrier, again leaned on Lydiard for work-outs. Michelson donned a pair of spikes himself and ran with his runners, trying to figure a way to minimize problems—psychological as well as physical—that can depress a runner and wear him down.

At that moment when his runners were about to suffer the vicissitudes of oxygen debt and other physiological changes in their bodies that could take a toll, he would move in beside them, stride for stride.

The coach held the advantage, of course. He was fresh. But because he was, he could drag them past the barriers of fatigue. He talked as he ran. "Think about your hip carriage. Remember what can happen to the way your body reacts when you get tired. Forget the fatigue. Concentrate on form. Stay loose! Loose! Loose!"

The state meet brought Schemmel and Heidenreich together again. Schemmel, fearing no one, counted on the strategy he had used at the conference meet when he ran 4:17: Go from the beginning with a searing pace and burn the field off. After all, had he not passed the three-quarter mark in that race in 3:10? And then coasted in the final 440 yards with a 67? And were Heidenreich and Titze even close? No.

Heidenreich was puzzled. "Schemmel said he was going to run 4:10 at the state meet; let the whole world know it," says Heidi. "I said to myself and to Drake: 'There's no way he can run that fast. He's not in that kind of physical condition.'"

On a Thursday night in late May at Rapid City, the psychological warfare was building. There were hundreds of athletes there for the state meet.

Michelson saw the fire in Heidenreich's eyes. "It was like he was saying, 'Hey, what's going on here?'" says the coach. "He didn't run the mile until Saturday but I wasn't bothered. He was ready."

Saturday. Race day. The day rose, brisk and hazy. At the track there was anticipation. The first lap of the mile was super-quick, the way Schemmel wanted it. The time was 57.2. Schemmel was a step behind the leader. Heidi and Titze were far back. The three-quarter time was 3:09 and Schemmel was in the lead by such a margin that the crowd stood and cheered. They thought the race was over.

Schemmel's torrid pace had put him in position to break contact with Heidenreich, and he felt comfortable. But on the first turn of the final lap, fatigue forced him to labor. His legs felt useless. The last quarter lasted forever.

"On the backstretch I totally dropped my anchor," said Schemmel afterward. "It's a shock when it happens because you don't expect it and there's not a damn thing you can do. All of a sudden your legs are gone and you are struggling to take your next step."

Schemmel had paid an awful price for his hard, fast pace. Heidenreich, sensing that Schemmel was straining, surged. ("You could just see it on the backstretch," says Michelson. "Heidenreich seemed to be saying, 'Yeah, I know you're a long ways out there but I also know I can still get you because I'm really feeling good and here I come!' You could just see that in his body.") Steadily, Heidi's pumping legs chewed up the gap and he overtook Schemmel. Heidi didn't dare look around; he was afraid he would stumble. Heidi snapped the tape and won in 4:16, a personal record. It was the first time he had beaten Schemmel. Titze also caught Schemmel and finished second in 4:21.1.

Michelson, sitting in the stands, was not there long. "I busted out of my seams with happiness," he says. "Coaches weren't supposed to be on the infield but I got out there."

Michelson and Heidenreich and Titze, with their arms around each other, danced for joy. The coach wept unashamedly.

"On that day, Heidi found it," says Michelson. "He found what he was really seeking and all of the things fell right into the bag."

On that day, Steve Heidenreich distinguished the real from the abstract. The watch, stopped at 4:16, displayed tangibly what he had been privately musing: that he might be a better runner than he had ever before dared to believe possible.

"I ran a smart race," said Heidenreich in recalling the episode later. "I ran smart and I ran an even pace and I beat him. I knew that he couldn't run 4:10. I knew the best I could run was 4:16. Well, that's what I did. He tried to run his 4:10 but he broke down.''

It was then that Heidenreich, a high school junior, arrived at a startling discovery.

''. . . I knew I could break four minutes in a mile,'' he says. ''I knew it that day.''

He told this to no one then. The astounding realization that he might be able to run that fast, to shatter what once was an unapproachable barrier, was his secret.

Years later, he said: ''In fact, I was surprised it took me so long. [On May 3, 1975, he ran a 3:59.6 in a triangular meet among Indiana, Western Kentucky, and Bowling Green.] If I hadn't been hurt so often in college I would have done it sooner.''

At the conclusion of the 1970 track season in May, Heidenreich's optimism was unbridled and his confidence sure. He had tasted success. ''Running was fun,'' he says, ''because I knew then I was going to be very good.''

Heidenreich and Titze still ran together that summer of 1970. They watched each other carefully, like poker players surreptitiously sizing up the others at the table. They wanted to be together because it was hard not to be. They shared thoughts and sought psychological advantages. There was mutual respect. ''Track was important to me,'' says Titze, ''but I had many other things, too. Track was Steve's life. Period. He was driven.''

Intrinsically shy, Heidi kept all but his family at a distance. ''He was a different type of guy,'' says Roger Konrady, a shot-putter and an all-state football player, in gauging his friend. ''He wasn't the type to get real close to anyone; he wasn't somebody you could confide in and yet I felt like I was almost as close to him as anyone.

''He didn't party a whole lot. A bunch of us would go over to this kid's garage and lift weights and then go to get beer. He'd say, 'No, I gotta run.' He wouldn't do anything if it interfered with his workout. He wanted to be number one and the number one thing with him was his running.''

Heidenreich became a familiar figure on the streets of Watertown and on the shoulder of Highway 20, or in the ditches, on his way out to Lake Kampeska. Running. Running. Running. His clergyman, Pastor Fischer, would shake his head in wonder. "Sometimes the boy was in church and he'd be limping and his knees were big and puffy. I remarked to people that I thought his career as a runner had kind of gone down the drain because the boy was plain running his legs off."

Heidi would smile. "I'm good," he told his pastor. "You know I'm good and I know I'm good."

That summer, Heidenreich and Vic Michelson spent hours together painting the coach's house. Michelson had offered him the job and said he'd pay him by the hour. Heidi held out for more money and won. During lemonade breaks under a large tree in the yard they talked.

Heidi said to Michelson one afternoon, "Coach, you know we should be tougher; some of those guys we run against are gutless. We should be working harder."

Michelson sighed at his protégé's enthusiasm. "Be patient. I think we can."

Vic knew Steve was a bright student. As they talked he purposely shifted the conversation away from running to see what other thoughts were clicking in his young runner's mind. Independent and insular by nature, Steve did not feel comfortable in large groups. And unless asked, he talked of little else than track. His shyness made him appear masked when he was not, and he appeared not terribly deep inside.

"What would you like to do with your life, Steve?" asked Michelson.

"I don't know. Maybe psychology. Maybe drama. Maybe dentistry. I've thought about all three."

He took a psychology course that stirred him. He was captivated by the study of the mind and a person's behavioral tendencies. He was one of the few students to ask discerning questions. But, surprisingly, he did not display the abundant drive in the classroom that he did on the track. He appeared in dramatic productions, losing himself in the creativity. He thought drama to be a beautiful way to express himself, to say some things he wanted to say, without having to come outside the wall with which he had surrounded himself.

They ran together, the coach and his pupil, becoming close friends. It was then that Michelson began to perceive a restlessness, a rebellion in his runner.

So, too, did cross-country coach Dwight Struckman. The day before Watertown's first cross-country meet of the season, Struckman handed out jerseys to his team. Heidenreich, among the last to pick up his, instructed: "I want number one."

"Steve, that number was handed out long ago," said Struckman. Steve swore.

"Listen, we don't swear in the locker room. I don't swear. It's school policy not to." Heidi should have remembered. The previous fall he had cursed during a workout at the golf course. Those guilty of such a malfeasance were required by Struckman to do pushups. "I didn't run that day," says Heidi. "I was on the ground the whole time doing pushups."

After the season began, Heidenreich visited Struckman at his home.

"I want to fix up my own workouts," said Heidi.

"That's a little unusual," said Struckman. "I suppose it's okay if you bring them to me to be approved."

"I don't like anyone telling me what to do."

"Steve, you've got to realize that no matter what you do as you get older, you're going to have someone over you, someone else in authority."

"Not me. I'm going to be a psychologist. They have their own say-so."

Shortly thereafter, an order was passed from the athletic director to Struckman: No one on the cross-country team was to wear his meet shorts to practice.

Another clash ensued.

Struckman's punishment for those who disobeyed was to wear sweat bottoms at workouts. Heidenreich walked out of the locker room one afternoon with his meet shorts on. Struckman stopped him.

"Steve, you know what the rule is," said the coach.

"I'm not running in any sweats."

"Well, it's your choice. You either run in sweat bottoms or you don't run."

"I'm not running." The silence that followed was deafening.

Heidenreich, exasperated and in a snit, never returned. The runner who presumably would have been the South Dakota cross-country champion chose not to run.

Michelson, a football line coach that autumn, watched Heidi's explosion closely. "There was anxiety and hostility there," recalls Michelson. "I really believed that if he could have gotten to a race car he would have entered the Indianapolis 500 and there would have been no fear on his part. None. His life was so hurried then and he was searching."

Steve stuck by his decision; no cross-country. He continued to run on his own, however. When the spring track season came, Heidi bumped into another old inflicter of retribution: Jeff Schemmel, who beat him in their first three duels, the latter at the Watoma Relays in Watertown.

Michelson was greatly disturbed by the feedback that filtered down to him from those who had watched the race from the stands. "Well, that's it for Heidenreich," they said. "He'll never beat Schemmel again." Michelson was inspired to do something different, and called Heidi to come see him.

"Steve," said the coach, "we're going to do it my way now. You'll not run against Schemmel again until the conference meet and when you do, you'll be ready for him."

The race, Michelson figured, would be decided on the third lap. He prepared grueling interval workouts. When Heidi came to practice the next Monday, Michelson was waiting.

"Today we will run a 440, rest one minute and then run an 880, all at race pace," said the coach. Heidi rose from his stretching and walked to the starting point. The track at Watertown Stadium is not artificial surface, it's made of cinders. Heidi ran. Michelson stood with a watch in his hand, gazing closely at his runner, whose torso was erect and his arms pumping. The coach called out the times.

"Sixty-one! Rest and we'll go."

Heidi ran.

"Two-o-five! Rest and we'll go." A 440. An 880. A 440. An 880.

On the following night, Michelson flip-flopped the schedule. Heidi ran first an 880 and then a 440. The sets were repeated. On the next night, Michelson talked softly with his runner.

"We must run hard 220s. Twenty-five of them and none slower than 27 seconds."

Heidi ran. He trudged across the football field to the starting point, watched for the signal from his coach and, again, began his sprint.

The workouts were relentless but with purpose. Day after day after day. Heidi, a film of perspiration covering his face, listened to his coach.

"Okay, now this is the quarter where we beat Schemmel, the third quarter, let's go to work on it. Let's get tough." Heidi ran quarters. Michelson, with the watch, called them off:

"Sixty! . . .

"Fifty-nine! . . .

"Fifty-eight! . . .

"Sixty-two! . . .

"Sixty!"

Heidi ran. Again. And again. And again. The rest of the team watched in amazement each day. Every day. The days rolled on.

Michelson could see Heidi's speed improving. "He never complained," said the coach later. "Those workouts were fierce, far beyond what I thought many could stand, but he was ready for more and he got more."

Heidenreich, blasting a set of 220s, had no idea what his capacity was. Expressionless, he sprinted—springily, strongly. His lungs felt as if they would burst. He heard Michelson call out the time.

"Twenty-six four!"

Heidi was ready. The weather on the day of the conference meet at Yankton was perfect: No breeze, warm, sunny. Michelson told Heidenreich to settle in behind Schemmel for the first half-mile and on the third lap to push the pace. The third lap, the lap when they would go for it.

Schemmel, as usual, took control from the gun, running fluidly through a 2:06 the first 880. At the start of the third lap, Heidenreich spurted and seized the inside lane. Schemmel sat on his shoulder. They were yelling up in the stands. Heidi, his mouth dry, was saying to himself, "Here it is. Here it is."

Michelson describes the fourth lap:

"Heidi made his break and Schemmel went with him and she was a race . . . she sure was. They ran stride-for-stride on the backstretch until they came into the last turn."

Michelson, from his seat in the stands, bellowed:

"Don't let him get ahead of you! Don't let him cut in!"

Heidi never heard him. The roar of the crowd had drowned out Michelson's plea. Heidenreich pushed again, harder still. The positions did not change in their headlong rush for the tape. Heidi snapped it first; Schemmel was a step back. The winning time was 4:11.2, faster than any miler, high school or collegian, had ever run in South Dakota. It was history. Schemmel, who ran 4:12.2, embraced Heidenreich, an unusual gesture since these two had coldly avoided each other as their rivalry had mushroomed.

Michelson was euphoric. He threw his clipboard into the air and, hurdling a snow fence that circled the track, grabbed Steve Heidenreich and swept him up.

Steve's parents had watched with characteristically quiet Heidenreich pride the development of their son as a runner. But their attention to him was not at the expense of their other children who also were achieving, Linda academically and Roger as a high-school debater. Heidi's parents saw almost every one of his races in high school and once DeLoris drove Steve and Drake Titze to a meet in a Minnesota town 250 miles away when they missed the team bus. Merle became so wrapped up in Steve's running that he began jogging daily.

Heidi's life was about to change. Any high-school runner with times like his attracts the attention of college recruiters. The phone calls and visits began. Nebraska. Missouri. Indiana. Villanova. LSU. They all wanted to woo him.

Two days before the state meet was held at Sioux Falls, a telegram was delivered to the Heidenreich house from the two track and field coaches at the University of Missouri, Tom Botts and Bob Teel. It said:

STEVE STOP BEST OF LUCK TO YOU, DRAKE,
COACH MICHELSON AND YOUR TEAM STOP

At that state meet, in a blustery wind that was hitting as high as forty miles an hour, Heidenreich hooked up with Schemmel in what was billed by sportswriters as the Dream Mile, a title they had taken from a thrilling race (also called the Dream Mile) that had been run a few days previously in Philadelphia and had been televised nationally. In it, Marty Liquori had beaten Jim Ryun.

The wind blunted any attempt by either Heidenreich or Schemmel to run under 4:10, blowing, as it was, in their faces on the home stretch side of the track. The pace was far from hot. When the runners, all strong, fit, and not prepared for anything spectacular, swung into the final lap Heidenreich took the lead and Titze came up on Schemmel's outside shoulder and boxed him in. "I shoved my way out of there," recalls Schemmel. "I hit Drake—I got out of there quick." Schemmel caught Heidenreich but could not stay with him. Heidi kicked a stinging 56-second final 440. "We hit that backstretch and he just ran away from me," says Schemmel. "I thought, 'My God, he's killing me and I'm running hard.' "

Heidenreich, meanwhile, was entranced. Never before had he felt this way—as though he had total control over every movement his body was making. "The wind was at my back and I knew I had the race won and, I mean, I was high. I felt so light on my legs; I was moving quickly. When I came around and the wind was blowing at me it was nothing because victory was already there and my body wasn't paying for anything."

Heidi's time was 4:23.4. Schemmel (4:25.7) was second.

Standing on the infield, Michelson shook hands with his two runners. Enormously proud, there was no way he could have made either Steve or Drake understand the gratitude he was feeling.

There was little time for Steve Heidenreich to think. He made a recruiting visit to Indiana University, returned home and announced to his family that he had made his choice: He would become a Hoosier. Transplanted, of course.

"He had proved that he could run with anyone in cold climate," says Michelson. "Indiana was warmer, the coach sounded like a nice guy and the school had good facilities. He'd lean that way and then he'd want more questions answered."

Heidi was invited to run in the All-American High School Track and Field Championships in Lombard, Illinois, a suburb of Chicago. It was a meet that brought the best of the country's preps together. The Watertown Quarterback Club paid his expenses.

The sun was boiling on June 12, 1971, the day of the meet. In that sweltering heat Heidi ran second in 4:11.8 behind Mike Durkin of Chicago, who did 4:09.4.

Durkin was a runner who, like Heidi, was courageous and strong and about to become his inexorable rival. He would eventually win the prize that Heidi coveted the most.

Heidenreich and Vic Michelson parted. "He looked at Indiana University and he told me, 'Here's what I think I can do; here's what I'd like to do.' There was no question in my mind or his that he would be a sub-four-minute miler some day."

They both were right.

4

Wednesday. A September day. Indian summer in southern Indiana. During the night a rain had washed the streets of Bloomington and now, as the city began to stir, there was the promise of a clear, pure day ahead.

The electric alarm clock near Steve's bed pierced the silence in his dormitory room. Without even opening his eyes he could stick out his left hand and shut it off. The first week he arrived at Indiana University he had taught himself to position the clock where he could reach it with the least amount of effort.

For a moment he lay motionless. Then he rolled over, grabbed the clock and looked at it—6:30, right on the button. He rose stiffly and took a few steps to the bedside of his roommate, Steve Weiss.

"Steve! Wake up! . . .

"C'mon! . . .

"Let's go!"

Heidenreich shook Weiss. No response.

He flicked Weiss's ear.

"A-R-R-R-G-H-H . . .!"

Weiss looked up with a befuddled expression on his face and was greeted by Heidi's disarming smile.

Thwock.

A pillow sailed in Heidenreich's direction, aimed specifically at his nose. Heidi ducked. The pillow smacked against the wall and landed on a pair of Nike training flats. It was evident that runners lived here. Nike and Adidas shoes were arranged in orderly rows along one wall. On doorknobs and on the backs of chairs running shorts, T-shirts, nylon windbreakers and warmup jackets were hung to dry.

Heidi had arrived in Bloomington with little fanfare. He shyly examined this new world that awaited him and found a sense of communion among the other IU track team members. They were from all across the nation but as runners they were similar: They liked to race hard and they hated to lose.

Heidenreich's 4:11.2 was the thirteenth fastest time by a high-school miler in the United States in 1971. Mike Durkin's 4:08.3 was third and Jeff Schemmel's 4:12.2 was eighteenth. Weiss's marathon time of 2:39:47 was tenth among high-school runners.

The zeal with which Heidenreich pursued his new life-style was typical. Independent now, he managed the transition from the family nest in Watertown with ease. The anxieties that tormented him the previous year had disappeared. There were now other things in his life in addition to running, some of which he had no choice about. The most significant of these were the books—his academic obligations. His studies were focused on a career in dentistry.

Curiously, Heidi made a rapid 180-degree turnabout. He was changed. He no longer marched to his own drum. His unbending stubbornness vanished. He wanted to be surrounded by laughter and, likewise, he surrounded his friends with laughter.

Each morning Heidenreich ran with Weiss. Sometimes their steps took them on sidewalks through the campus. Sometimes they followed a road that led them to the outskirts of town. Sometimes they ran through the wet grass and boldly scaled the demanding hills of IU's golf course, the site of the Hoosiers' home cross-country meets. It was an arduous layout that, measured by degree of difficulty, was one of the nation's better tests for collegiate runners.

On this day they selected a twisting route that took them through Cascades Park, a small, quaint roadside pass which would surprise any motorist who came unexpectedly upon it. Lined by tall shade trees, the park area was walled on one side by an outcropping of rock. Beneath this wound a narrow, sinuous creek.

Heidenreich and Weiss ran with long, soundless strides. They avoided the mud borders along the roads that were mushy from the previous night's rain. Their steps quickened as they ran downhill into the park and then, almost as fast as they had entered this small sanctuary, they were out of it and crossing Highway 37, narrow at this point but heavily traveled.

Leaving the highway, Heidenreich and Weiss turned to their right and began an upward trek on first a steep incline and then a hill of lesser grade, the two together tackling a climb that left them gasping of anoxia and gulping oxygen. Recovery, on a long, flat stretch of Dunn Street, was just ahead—and welcome.

As Heidi and Weiss were running on Dunn, a residential street, Heidenreich said, "Watch this." A car slowed to give the runners room and as Heidi ran alongside it he rapped a fender with his knuckles and then tumbled into the grass of an adjacent yard with his hands wrapped around his knee, screaming:

". . . Oh, my leg! Oh! Oh!"

The driver slammed on his brakes and rushed to the side of the fallen Heidenreich.

"For Chrissakes, kid, I'm sorry," said the driver, his voice quivering.

"Are you all right?"

"Sure!" announced Heidenreich, bouncing up and jogging away as the man, astonished, could only stare.

Heidi the prankster was not to be so lucky during the first three years of his college career. The young runner who had always prided himself on his fitness was now beset with illness and injuries.

He missed a lot of his freshman track season, indoor and outdoor, and metatarsal injuries cost him part of his indoor season as a sophomore. During his junior cross-country season he developed painful chondromalacia, the softening of cartilage in the undersurface of the kneecap. Heidi was pushing himself much too hard in his training.

The body must adapt to the stresses of distance running. The bones of the foot and lower leg, through the repeated stress of the pounding that 1,500 to 1,600 steps a mile can produce, can develop minute breaks called stress fractures. Rest is the accepted cure. The stresses of running also can cause abnormal movement and wear on the kneecap and the end of the femur, the upper leg bone. Sometimes the misalignment of the bone and kneecap, which causes a grinding action during running, is the fault of the stresses of footplant on uneven surfaces—sides of hills or roads with high crowns which naturally put one foot lower than the other. Rest and reduced running on grassy surfaces usually clears up the condition. Chondromalacia is a common disorder among runners.

"A great runner has both mental and physical toughness," explains Sam Bell, Steve's coach at IU. "Heidi is a frail type and it took him a long time to understand that there were limits to what he could do in training; that he could not do the volume of work that, say, a Steve Prefontaine could and survive. It's why Heidi was injured so much."

Bell guided Heidenreich through that period of precarious balancing when he wasn't healthy and wanted desperately to be. A sensitive, forthright man, Bell made his track and field team a part of his family. "If they are anything less you probably aren't putting into it what you ought to," he once said. "When you coach, you coach people. The sport is incidental. I went into coaching because I saw it as an avenue to reach young people. And an avenue to influence them, too. I could tell when we recruited Steve Heidenreich that he was strong willed. We had tried to recruit Mike Durkin also and *he* sure wasn't passive. They both knew what they wanted to accomplish."

As a coach, Bell was both no-nonsense and paternalistic in his approach. And a winner. Educated at Doane College in Crete, Nebraska, and at the University of Oregon, he was the coach of the United States team that riddled Russia in a dual meet, 139–97, in 1964. In 1976 he was the men's distance coach on the American staff for the Olympic Games at Montreal. His Oregon State University cross-country team won the NCAA championship in 1961. At Indiana he sprinkled a variety of aphorisms into his coaching philosophy. His athletes are always critiqued in a postmeet manifest. Those who did well find their names under the "Great Performance" category. Those who did poorly will be publicly remonstrated and assigned to the "Disappointment" category. But, always, the team is reminded by Sam Bell to:

(1) Bite down.

(2) Get competitive and perform with pride.

(3) Be intense.

(4) Dare to be great.

(5) Rid yourself of complacency.

Bell's athletes privately grumbled but they were anxious to please him, Heidi among them. While Heidenreich was at IU he was a member of five Big Ten Conference championship track and field teams (indoor and outdoor) and two conference cross-country championship teams. Never before had Indiana University known such success.

Sam Bell applied all of his principles double strength to ready his freshman, Steve Heidenreich, for his first collegiate race. This was on September 18, 1971, at the IU golf course in a dual cross-country meet with Indiana State University. Heidenreich ran five miles in 25:27 and was third.

Heidi did not falter that season. He finished as the number one runner on the team and in his first confrontation with Mike Durkin since their race on that muggy day in Lombard, Illinois, he ran with a vengeance.

Durkin had been forewarned. Bob Wright, then the Illinois coach, told him, "There's a boy at Indiana who said he's going to grind you into the dust. He said he's never going to lose to you again." Durkin was perplexed. Who? "Heidenreich," Wright told him. "You beat him at the All-America meet, remember?" Durkin hadn't known the name of the runner who had finished behind him in that race, but he surely would never forget the Heidi who handed him a convincing defeat in a six-mile race over the hills at Bloomington. Heidi was second in 31:01.5. Durkin was 25th in 34:14.

Bell was ecstatic. His comment to Heidi on the postmeet sheet

said: "I can't really say enough about the way you are performing. It's gotten to a point where I expect a super performance
from you each time out because that's what you give. You beat
Mike Durkin, a 4:09 high-school miler, by more than three minutes!" Durkin was not ever to be embarrassed in such enervating
fashion again.

In fact, Durkin won more than he lost in his head-to-head duels
with Heidenreich during their collegiate rivalry. Their competition became a matter of course as they fought bitterly in races at
Bloomington and at Champaign, Illinois, and in Big Ten championship meets.

But the fighting was part of the excitement for Steve Heidenreich. He expanded in other ways as his running improved, and
he started to develop a social life. He got in line with the rest of
the crowd waiting to get into Nick's, a local watering hole. It's
a popular place, usually filled with a boisterous crowd. At Nick's
one can buy beer by the mug or by the pound. And Heidi subscribed to the theory that beers were a must if you wanted to be
a good distance runner. On the ceiling above the bar are 140 tin
buckets for beer with the names of the owners painted in red. On
one wall is a large oil painting that originally depicted nudes in
an assortment of poses. Somebody with a paintbrush clothed
them. Festooning other walls are several *Playboy* centerfolds,
dented bugles, half an IU football helmet and the IU basketball
uniform (No. 35) that seven-footer Lou Scott wore when he
played in 1953.

Steve usually met his friends at Nick's after he finished studying at night and on the weekends. The social world that exists
at a major university was something Heidi, perhaps a bit naïve,
had never been exposed to. He stood, blinking, in horrified fas-
cination one night when a student was handcuffed and hustled
off by police on a drug charge at the entrance to his dorm while
the student's girlfriend screamed hysterically. The heavy use of
drugs and the many student protest groups shocked him.

Certainly, Steve Heidenreich's new world was in agreement
with him and he with it. As long as he was running well he was
content. His grade point average in his first semester was 3.3 on

a 4-point scale. Heidenreich possessed a new spirit: Scholarly, questioning, free, easy. He was given to infectious laughter, and wherever Heidi went, his roommate Weiss was sure to follow. They partied a lot. Heidi was the leader whether they spent an evening studying, planning a new running route, or walking downtown just to see what was going on.

One evening, finishing up a twilight run, Heidenreich and Weiss stopped at Cafe Pizzeria, a restaurant in downtown Bloomington. They ordered a small pepperoni. The waiter, a friend, returned to the table struggling with a monstrous pizza that was heaped with mushrooms, anchovies, peppers, bacon, sausage . . . well, everything but one of Sam Bell's stopwatches and one of Bob Knight's basketballs. Heidi's eyes twinkled.

"Eat, gluttons," ordered the waiter. "You'll never run again."

As a prophet, he could not have been more wrong.

And yet, Heidi did not run at all during the spring of 1972. A stress fracture of a metatarsal bone in his foot, a hairline break that was the result of a heavy running schedule, knocked him out of action. He was depressed and upset and it was with difficulty that he said bon voyage to Sam Bell when the coach left for the Olympic Games at Munich.

That summer, Heidi went home to Watertown and, healed physically and refreshed mentally, he worked hard. He was a lifeguard at a country club six miles from his home. He ran to his job and there he swam, taught, cleaned the pool and ran home in the evening. Some days he worked with his father in the fields near Watertown, lifting bales of hay onto the tractor-driven flatbed rigs. Steadily, he became stronger and stronger. When he returned to Indiana University in late August he was a marvelous union of muscle and speed. Sam Bell was astonished when he saw him moving along on the IU golf course on his first day back. The kid just might beat everyone, he thought.

On September 23, in the Hoosiers' second meet, a dual with Southern Illinois University's Salukis, Heidi began a sensational string of victories. Here is how the streak went:

—September 23. At Bloomington. Individual winner, Steve Heidenreich. Five miles. Time 25:24.2.

—September 30. At the University of Cincinnati. Individual winner, Steve Heidenreich. Five miles. Time 25:21. New course record.

—October 7. At Bloomington. Individual winner, Steve Heidenreich. Six miles. Time 30:26.5. New course record.

—October 14. At Oxford, Ohio. Individual winner, Steve Heidenreich. Six miles. Time 29:19.5. New course record.

—October 20. At Bloomington. Individual winner, Steve Heidenreich. Five miles. Time 25:09.6. New course record.

—October 27. At West Lafayette, Indiana (Purdue). Individual winner, Steve Heidenreich. Five miles. Time 23:45. New course record.

Six wins in a row and five course records. Heidi, lean-faced and intense, was self-confident to a point just short of cockiness. "I was super-tough both physically and mentally," he said years later, recalling the remarkable streak. "I don't think I ever was so strong or had so much faith."

Sam Bell, in an interview with Bob Hammel, sports editor of the Bloomington *Herald-Telephone,* called Heidenreich "one of the real premier cross-country runners in the nation—in a class with Dave Wottle [a gold medalist at Munich] and Steve Prefontaine."

At Oxford, Ohio, Heidenreich had smashed a course record that had belonged to Sid Sink, a former American record holder in the steeplechase. The coach at Miami of Ohio (in Oxford) had assured everyone days before the meet that there was no way Heidenreich could get the record. Bell relayed that statement to Heidi. It made him work harder.

The remainder of that season was something for the history books. That fall Heidi was as good as any Sam Bell ever coached in cross-country. "If Heidi had gone on he could have been the national champion that year. He was that good," Bell insists. But something happened to change all that.

It was the first week of November. Heidi was preparing for the Big Ten Conference championships at Iowa City, Iowa, with those six straight victories behind him. He took a break one Sunday afternoon for an outing with a friend, Julie. The two wrestled playfully and he flipped her over his shoulder. She landed awkwardly on her neck. Later, she developed severe headaches and was hospitalized, fearing she had broken a vertebra; and although she was fine, she was severely shaken.

Dan Hayes, a teammate of Heidenreich, roomed with him at the Big Ten championships and was really concerned about his mood. "There shouldn't have been anyone in the Big Ten who could stay with Heidi," says Hayes. "He'd been blowing people away. But by the time we got to the race he was a basket case. He had been up for four nights studying and worrying about Julie and going to the hospital to see her.

"I doubt that this specific incident hurt him for the rest of the season. He was nagged by injuries that would occur when he tried to come back too hard. You could always count on Heidenreich to run a great race but the problem was that he was hurt so much."

Heidenreich put no particular emphasis on his emotional state. He denied that anything was bothering him and blamed his performance on the vagaries of his training schedule. He felt after the Big Ten meet he lost the endurance base he had built.

Whatever the reason, he finished third in the Big Ten meet. Glenn Herold of the University of Wisconsin, establishing a course record, was the winner. Mike Durkin placed 28th. Sam Bell's postmeet sheet comment said:

> Steve Heidenreich, you showed real character in your last two miles. You and I and everyone who has seen you run this year knows you belong up there where Glenn Herold was. He ran a great race but there is no way he is better than you are. It was probably a great experience to build on and maybe the best thing that could have happened for a learning experience and getting to know yourself.

The coach was reminding Heidenreich that in distance running the one factor which usually separates the great from the good is cerebral. There must be extraordinary tenacity, total commitment. At the NCAA championships later in November, a six-mile race over the Glenbrook golf course in Houston, Heidi was way back in 130th place. In the 50th position and wearing the purple of Kansas State was Jeff Schemmel.

Heidi ran well all throughout the 1973 indoor and outdoor seasons, trimming his mile time to 4:03.6. He was scolded by his coach for easing up near the end of an indoor race. Bell's comment sheet said:

> The lack of effort at the finish by Steve Heidenreich was typical of a prima donna, not a champion. I never want to see a man with an IU shirt on do anything like that again. If you are to be a champion you must compete like one, win or lose on a given occasion!

Heidi got the message.

However, he was soon lavished with kind words by Bell, who was pleased when Heidi defeated Durkin in a preliminary heat of the mile in the Big Ten outdoor championships. Then, in the final, Heidenreich finished third with his 4:03.6 behind the winner, Ken Popejoy of Michigan State, who blazed a 3:59.2.

On a path strewn with an almost equal number of triumphs and frustrations, Steve Heidenreich plunged forward. He laughed unbelievingly at those who said that he would never find consistency in his running. He knew it would be there if—*if* he could avoid those damnable injuries.

The year 1974 gave him that opportunity. In February, an IU foursome of Dan Hayes, Pat Mandera, Phil Wysong and Heidi set a world indoor record in the four-mile relay. Heidenreich ran his anchor leg in 4:05.1. Four days later he broke the IU school record in the 1,000 with a 2:09. It was the first time he had ever run the event and an astounded Bell rewarded him with inclusion in his Great Performances category.

In April, Bell took his team south for its spring trip. In a race against the Florida Track Club's Byron Dyce, Heidi blitzed a 4:02.9. Of Heidenreich's tantalizing time, Bell wrote:

> Heidi, you were great. That kind of effort will build you for the future. You had moments when you didn't reach when Dyce went

by and then you came back tough. You must trust yourself enough to go after it when the challenge is there and hang on. I think you'll surprise yourself!

On successive weekends Heidi ran 4:02.3 and 4:01.3, the latter an IU record, and Bell saw the real potential for his protégé. He wrote:

The time of sub-four will be there when you have to have it to win. You must keep your confidence against all competitors.

The next weekend at Philadelphia at the Penn Relays Heidi did it—he anchored the Hoosiers' two-mile relay with a 3:59.5 split, kicking the last 440 in 58.5. The Hoosiers were fifth but Heidi finally had his sub-four time. His joy was tempered, though, by the fact that it had come on a relay leg with a running start and so it did not hold the same significance as a sub-four in an open race. Only when he broke the four-minute barrier in an open race would he feel like a legitimate sub-four-miler.

After a slowish 1:58 half-mile in a dual meet with the University of Michigan he came back the next week to run a 4:02.1 and obliterate Dave Wottle's track record at Bowling Green.

At the NCAA outdoor championships at Austin, Texas, Heidi finished his warmup for a preliminary heat of the mile. Jogging to the far reaches of the track, he sat silently for ten minutes, then headed for the starting line. As he shed his sweats, he heard his name being called and was surprised to see Jeff Schemmel lining up right next to him. Schemmel recalled later: "It was one of the great moments in all my days of track. We had not raced against each other on the track for two years and here they stuck us in the same heat. It must have been fate. We were standing right next to each other at the line. We looked at each other, laughed, shook hands and thought . . . 'Well, here we are again.' Steve ran exactly the same tactics as he had against me on that windy day in South Dakota.

"On the last quarter, Heidi just flew. He deliberately forced the pace and the rest of us couldn't go with him." Heidenreich's winning time in the heat was 4:05.3. Schemmel was sixth in

4:09.0. In the final the next day Heidenreich placed sixth in 4:03.1.

Heidi gazed across the track, taking it all in. He had finished sixth. Good, but not the best. That was what he wanted to be, wasn't it? The best. He had had a glimpse of it. He had run under four minutes and he had run tough in the NCAA meet. His confidence soaring, he turned abruptly and walked away from the meet, believing, fervently, that the best was yet to come.

5

The art of running the sub-four-minute mile is not the breathless, collapsing-unconscious-at-the-tape, supreme passion as it was once described by the world's first four-minute miler, Roger Bannister who ran a 3:59.4 on the Iffley Road track at Oxford, England, on May 6, 1954.

Hundreds upon hundreds of sub-four-minute miles have been run in the years since Bannister ran his, quashing the belief that it was physically impossible. Bannister's training was practically nothing when compared to today's standards. Rather, Bannister's breakthrough was like the collapse of a flood wall. The resultant torrent of sub-four-minute miles after his proved that it was only the mystique, a barrier in the mind that, once erased, could open limitless possibilities.

What does the ideal miler look like? There appears to be no perfect body type. Consider pint-sized Americans Joie Ray and Jim Beatty and the tall and slim Bannister and Jim Ryun of America. Glenn Cunningham, an American, New Zealand's Peter Snell, and Kenya's Kip Keino were of average height. New Zealand's John Walker has wide shoulders and thick thighs from which he derives tremendous power. Walker ran 3:49.4 in 1975, which was a world mile record. Perhaps the prototype runner of the future, combining strength, size and speed, is Alberto Juantorena of Cuba, called El Caballo "The Horse," who at Montreal in 1976 became the first in the Olympic Games to win both the 800 meters and 400 meters. He is six feet two inches and weighs 185 pounds.

Steve Heidenreich squeezed every bit he could out of his 130-pound body. He was so slender that he appeared to be a vertical hyphen when he flashed through the tape, but God had blessed him with speed. And his spirit was downright pugnacious.

Dan Visscher, a six-foot four-inch miler from Dearborn, Michigan, and Tom Burleson, another miler, both met Heidenreich in the autumn of 1974. The three were constantly comparing their thoughts on running.

"Vissch," Heidi would say.

"Yeah?"

"Vissch, you gotta be tough. You gotta be hard-core."

Visscher was smitten with Heidi's courage and performance. "He was very fast and he was very strong," he says. "When you run as fast as he was running you experience pain but you have to get beyond it, and that's what made Heidenreich a good runner . . . what makes anybody a good runner. They're able to concentrate on the race and not their feelings."

The pain simply can't be ignored. Maybe it should not be. It was Australia's Percy Cerutty, a running coach who trained Herb Elliott, who advised: "Thrust against pain. Pain is the purifier. Walk toward suffering. Love suffering. Embrace it."

Runners get used to their kind of pain or discomfort and know how much of it their bodies can tolerate. Runners are not bionic; they are no different from anybody else. They don't enjoy the discomfort of extreme fatigue. They recognize pain not as a form of heroic sacrifice but as an inevitable body function that has to be endured. Acceptance of discomfort is the first step in diminishing its effects, and this is what Cerutty was advocating.

Running is not, and should not be, always associated with pain. Visscher explains. "If you're out there concentrating on beating the next guy and doing what you want to do, then how you feel won't ever enter into what you are doing," he says. "Heidi also had the physical tools. I know a lot of runners who have the physical tools but they don't have the mental toughness, if that's what it should be called. I prefer to call it competitive instinct.

"A lot of guys got on Heidenreich's case about it because in a workout he would challenge a lot of people. He wasn't afraid of that. He wasn't afraid to race and there were times when he had races that he didn't think he was properly trained for. When he thought he was running well and he was fit he wasn't afraid of anyone. A lot of runners doubt their abilities, doubt their conditioning, doubt their talent. No one can be a quality runner if those things are going through a runner's mind. No one can."

Pain. There is not a runner anywhere, novice or skilled, who hasn't experienced it because of the physiological processes a person's body goes through when he is exercising vigorously. The pain barrier was almost never a roadblock for Heidenreich. The secret was control of the mind and, thus, what the mind was telling the body. The pain was rarely a problem when he was fit.

Not all runners can summon the courage to embrace the feelings of discomfort that are natural in a swift race. Heidi had the courage and he learned to relax while racing. When he relaxed, the pain—a result of muscles wound as tight as springs—eased. During a race his mind would constantly remind his muscles to let go.

"I just say, 'HEY, RELAX!' " Heidi once commented. "Make the run as easy as possible. But that's not all there is to racing because a runner has to stay in contact with the leader, not let him get too far in front. In some races it is very hard to relax, especially if one of your opponents throws in a quick 400 meters [a tactic popularized by European runners to break up a race]. That upsets your relaxation. You have to train for it."

Relaxation is achieved by accepting the discomfort without doubt or fear. Proper training does not guarantee success but at least makes it possible. There comes the instant in a race when the runner actually gets to choose victory or defeat, when his mental and physical courage either take control positively or he backs off and disintegrates. At that instant it is futile to try to put more speed into his legs or extra oxygen into his lungs. He is either mentally resilient and strong or he is not.

Training is as necessary in inuring the mind as it is in preparing the body physically. A runner could get by with less training daily if his mental tenacity did not soften. Physically, it is not difficult to run 100 miles weekly. Mentally, it is difficult to get out of bed at 6 A.M. practically every day of the year to train.

Another part of a distance runner's training is use of the weight room, but not with the thought of developing a body like Arnold Schwarzenegger's. Runners must use weights carefully.

When Visscher walked into the IU weight room one afternoon after ten miles out on the roads he cautioned Heidenreich, who was working out furiously in one corner.

"Those aren't the exercises we're supposed to be doing," said Visscher, bewildered. "Aren't you lifting too much weight?"

"It makes me tough, Vissch. No Bs, no Gs."

"No . . . what?"

"No B-e-e-e-e-s, no G-e-e-e-e-s. No balls, no glory. Remember that, Vissch. You gotta be tough."

Visscher stared hard at his friend and suddenly saw why Heidi was no ordinary athlete. He was going to make it, and make it big. "Deep down inside Heidenreich believes he is good," says Visscher. "Some runners get that sensation once a season. They might be running out on the golf course and doing well and they'll say to themselves, 'Hey, I can be damn good,' and it will end there. They will create doubts. They're too tall or too skinny, or anything—just to have an excuse instead of concentrating.

"It is the ability to believe in yourself; to really, in a way, love yourself. Heidi loves what he is, what he can make of himself and a lot of people mistook that as being arrogant, and they resented it. I always found Heidenreich a very simple person, very up-front and unaffected. He had no inhibitions about being himself. I found him a sweet person and I liked to be with him because he made me feel good. Maybe it was telepathy. His confidence seemed to be transfused into me and I was more sure of myself."

The narcissism that Visscher perceived in Heidenreich was real. This attitude is esthetic and an important part of running. Ego-fulfillment is a positive force in a runner's drive to reach the goals he has set for himself.

Heidenreich never took an impersonal approach toward his opponents. If anything, he seemed to cultivate vendettas. His verbal thrusts were abrasive. He was imperious and often came on as brusque and testy. "When he was on the line it was him and a bunch of individuals he was racing against," says Visscher. "Of almost anybody he raced against he would say, 'I don't care what time he can run, the guy's got no guts!'" Mike Durkin, a bullish miler whose competitive frenzy was such that he acquired the sobriquet The Mad Durk, became Heidi's hottest foe. "Mike and I had a lot of respect for each other," says Heidenreich. "We were tough."

On March 8, 1975, at the Big Ten indoor championships in Bloomington, Heidi and Durkin clashed in a thrilling skirmish, one which the press had been writing about for a week before the event. Durkin was heavy with a chest cold and walking around like a zombie. What he wanted was a "sit-and-kick" mile. The runners passed the half-mile in 2:07 ("Somebody upstairs is rooting for me," thought Durkin). Then Durkin put Heidenreich in a box and shrewdly kept him there, a ploy that cost Durkin a few extra yards of running but kept the pace slow as he had wanted.

Durkin strode alongside Heidi and stayed there. Heidenreich was unable to squirt through on the inside, could not force his way out and could not back off and go on the outside because the other runners were on his heels. Durkin surged with 440 yards left and Heidi went with him. The two milers dashed the final lap and the slim margin that Durkin had seized earlier he held onto. His winning time was 4:05.5. Heidi ran 4:05.9.

Weekends at the Beta Theta Pi house were a relief from the grueling schedule. When Heidi was in an ebullient mood his whims were likely to result in outlandish odysseys. One of these adventures took Heidi and a carload of friends, on a whim, from Bloomington to Cincinnati for the second game of a Reds' doubleheader. Arriving home at 4 A.M. Heidi slipped into bed just in time to beat the morning chirps of the birds in the trees that stood guard around the Beta house. That morning, Heidi, his energy so

excessive, ran a 4:03 mile, a feat which, considering the circumstances, left all who knew of his previous evening sojourn stu-
pefied.

May. The Bloomington days, unseasonably mild, grew longer,
driving thousands of sun-worshiping students to the parks and to
the beaches of Lake Monroe, a massive, wandering reservoir
southeast of town in the lush Hoosier National Forest. Heidi
found some escape here from his uncompromising daily training,
but even so he was driving himself. Each night at 10 or 10:30 he
would run alone. In the afternoons he would work at the track.
Some days he would run twelve or more 400s in 58 seconds,
each with a very short rest in between. Some days he would
alternate 220s and 880s and 110s, sharpening his speed. He was
fit. He was not afraid to push himself to the limit.

As the weather grew warmer several of the runners brought a
dollar to practice each day and afterward they would jog to the
Penguin, a drive-in that served huge, thick malts which put Heidi
in a state of rare bliss. "Fantastic," he would say, stretching his
legs out on a bench while he wrestled with the straw. "Look at
the strawberries! So big I need a spoon. Get me a spoon, somebody. These are dynamite. Like having a beer."

Powered by Penguins, Heidenreich began a remarkable series
of four meets in a period of twenty-one days in which he placed
himself among the elite of America's collegiate milers. Here is the
way they went:

—*At Bloomington.* A 4:00.3. It was a school record for the
event. He celebrated with a Penguin.

—*At Bowling Green, Kentucky.* A 3:59.6 in a loss to Western Kentucky's Nick Rose, an Englishman who ran 3:59.0.
It was the first sub-four-minute mile ever run within the
environs of the state of Kentucky and it gave Heidi what he
wanted: A sub-four in an open race. He now could consider
himself a legitimate sub-four-minute miler. He was the first
in Indiana University history and the third in his history of
the Big Ten Conference to run that fast.

—*At Iowa City, Iowa.* The Big Ten outdoor championships.
A 4:05.3 for his first conference individual title. He became

IU's first conference mile champion in thirty-three years.
—At Manhattan, Kansas. A 3:59.6 in the Kansas State Invitational and a track record. In fifth place was K-State's Jeff Schemmel at 4:03.6.

Heidi was now on top of the world. He was tough and getting tougher every weekend. He considered himself ready to step up a notch into the fraternity of international-class milers. He was ready to bloom. The Manhattan race had been easy and after it was over he felt hardly fatigued. "It happens that way after a very successful race," he once said. "There wasn't much work to it and you wonder why you can't do it all the time. The big thing is that I was relaxed. I ran easy, I ran relaxed. Take two runners of almost equal ability and the one who runs fast but relaxed will in most cases win."

Schemmel brought Heidenreich to his house after the meet and there they partied far into the night. Beer, the water of life for distance runners, flowed. They relived their high school races and buried forever the bitterness that had flared then. And they indulged in the craze that was sweeping the nation. They streaked.

Returning to the motel at dawn, Heidenreich slept for forty-five minutes and then joined teammates Tom Burleson and Dean Reinke for a morning run. They got lost and almost missed their plane. Reinke, a distance runner, roomed with Heidi for one week at Fort Collins, Colorado, where they trained in the high altitude for the upcoming NCAA outdoor championships at Brigham Young University in Provo, Utah. The two had complemented each other as leaders on the Indiana team, Heidi espousing a hard-line approach and Reinke a softer one.

Reinke admired Heidenreich, knowing full well that those who were counted by Heidi in his close circle of friends had really earned his respect. Steve Heidenreich was wary of friendships; a stranger had to prove his worth and a runner had to prove his courage. Once Heidi was convinced of both he lowered his guard and his friendship was solid.

Heidi and Reinke were lying on their motel beds in Colorado, lazily gazing at the ceiling.

"You know what I don't want at Provo?" Heidenreich asked.
"What."

"Leeches," he answered with heavy sarcasm. "Those guys
who suck in behind you and make you do all the work. They
never take the lead, they wait and wait for you to die and then
you're lookin' at their heels. I want it to be a real race."

It was. Ireland's Eamonn Coghlan, a student at Villanova University, sprinted past Texas-El Paso's Wilson Waigwa, a Kenyan,
on the final curve of the mile. Waigwa could not respond. San
Jose State's Mark Schilling and Heidenreich began to move. But
a fast qualifying mile the day before had drained Heidi and bound
up his legs. Schilling closed to within two yards of Coghlan when
he hit the "wall," that imaginary barrier when a runner suddenly
feels bilious and his legs are like lead.

Each . . . Step . . . Becomes . . . Drudgery.

Across the finish line they flew, Coghlan first, followed by
Schilling, Waigwa, and Heidenreich, who ran 4:02.24 with a
58.9 for the last 440 yards.

Steve Heidenreich had finished as the second-highest American in the race at Provo and he had improved his position in the
NCAA championships from his sixth place of the previous year.
From Provo Heidi went to Berkeley, California, for the Meet of
Champions, where Waigwa surprised everyone with a sudden
surge and won by an eyelash. Waigwa's time was 4:00.6. Heidi
was second in 4:00.7, followed by Mike Durkin (4:01.1) and
Marty Liquori (4:01.6). Next up for Heidi was America's national
championships, the AAU meet, at Eugene, Oregon. The NCAA
meet is the collegiate championship and, as such, it includes
foreign athletes who are students in American universities. Many
of the same foreigners run in the AAU meet, which is open to all,
even though it is this nation's real championship. The AAU meet
is considered the more prestigious and any athlete who wants to
compete on an American team abroad during the summer
months must do well in the AAU meet.

The day dawned overcast in Eugene and the skies, often azure,
were leaden. Early in the morning a soft rain had fallen, soaking
the pine trees in the foothills that rim this college town. The old,

green wooden stands at Hayward Field on the edge of the University of Oregon campus were full of spectators for the AAU meet. They were eager but not enthusiastic. Eugene, the most running-conscious town in the United States, had recently lost the young runner whose name had already become a legend. It would be difficult for the crowd to find a replacement so soon for Steve Prefontaine.

He was a thick-chested Olympian from nearby Coos Bay who raged publicly at restrictions placed on American runners by the AAU. "Pre's People," his following, felt he had charisma. They would begin gathering at the track early when he was to run, just to watch him lope through an easy warmup. His races followed an exciting pattern. He would throw a lung-searing pace at his opponents and arrogantly dare them to meet the challenge.

And when, with his head cocked to one side, he quickened the pace on the final lap of Hayward Field's tan-colored track, exploding into a beautiful stride that was both fast and powerful, his legions would roar, rising to their feet and shaking their fists. When it was over, after Pre had run through the tape, the crowd would stream out of the seats and surround him and demand an autograph or a pat on their son's head. Pre, his chest heaving, would do as they asked. These were his people.

On this day of the AAU meet the mood of the crowd was subdued. One month before, in May 1975, Prefontaine had been killed when his MG had flipped, throwing him free, landing on top of him and crushing his chest and stomach. Hours before he had run the second-fastest three-mile ever by an American at Hayward Field in a meet with visiting athletes from Finland. Later, at a party, he had consumed quantities of beer in the best European post-race tradition and he talked of going to Helsinki to compete. The accident report showed his blood alcohol level to be .160 percent, too high to drive without impairment. The anguish of his death still gripped Eugene. Many people in the crowd at Hayward Field on this day had been there at a memorial service and remembered that Frank Shorter had said: "He was somebody I held in awe, not for the times he ran but for the way he ran, all out. Steve did not associate with me in a close manner until I had shared the lead with him in a three-mile race. It was as if I had passed some sort of test. He thought it was only right that I should help with the pace. I did, and then I was his friend."

The crowd was restrained on this chilly day, perhaps remembering their former hero, until the pack of runners in the 1,500, bunched and dangerously close to each other, moved into the curve as the bell clanged for the last 400 meters. Suddenly, an electricity was passed from one person to another in the crowd.

Sensing a rousing finish, the people stood and shrieked. This was a Pre race and the lean runner with the hair flying behind who had popped into the lead reminded them a little of him. His name was Steve Heidenreich.

Heidi swung wide of the edge of the track and shut his eyes, squeezing out the pain. He could feel the breathing behind him.

"Go now!" he told himself.

Heidenreich accelerated. He opened a gap of three yards but he could not hold it. He forced himself, trying to run faster. It took all he had just to hold on. But his energy reserve was being depleted and his legs were beginning to tie up, to tighten.

He had sprinted too soon. All he had left was his will to fight. Weakening, he was passed by one runner . . . then another . . . and another. The crowd was howling. He had run the final 320 yards in 42.9 seconds and scattered many in the field behind him but not enough in front.

He had finished fourth in 3:40.2. Nevertheless, those who left Hayward Field in the twilight made a mental note of the guy wearing the crimson and cream of Indiana University. He certainly fit Steve Prefontaine's motto: He could stand the pain and he could play the game.

His 3:40.2 was the equivalent of a 3:57 mile, faster than he had run in his life. His breakthrough was due to the high quality of the field. But even as fit as he was, this did not guarantee him a first place in every race. Middle-distance and distance running is not measured in the same units as some other sports. Consider basketball. There are many different ways to score a basket, and the player is dependent on his teammates for help. There is one way to run fast. That is fast. And alone.

Consider also the mutable qualities of racing. No one can wind up a runner with a key and instruct: "Today you will run four minutes." The weather, the tactics, the state of his mind, his physical condition, the abilities of the other runners—all of these can determine why a runner wins one day and is fourth the next, particularly if most of the runners in a race are of almost equal talent.

The reward for the winner of the 1,500 at Eugene was a place on the American team for a dual meet with the Soviet Union at Kiev. The winner, Len Hilton, could not go because of other commitments. Ken Popejoy, who was second and was a former Big Ten rival of Heidenreich, could make the trip. Mark Schilling, who was third, and Heidi both came to Popejoy to ask him if he would be going to Russia. When Popejoy said yes, he would make the trip, Heidi looked away. "I could tell he was thinking, 'Well, that's great for you but I wish you weren't going and I was,'" recalls Popejoy.

It was a bittersweet Steve Heidenreich who left Eugene to return to Bloomington to enroll in summer school. Elated that he had run one of the best races of his life at Eugene but disappointed that his track season was over.

What surprises awaited him.

6

Tuesday afternoon. Muggy. Sticky. Under the tranquilizing June sun the city of Bloomington was redolent with summer foliage. Steve Heidenreich had switched his academic major from dentistry to business and was taking courses in summer school.

In the intervening days following Heidenreich's departure from Eugene the meet between Russia and the United States had been scrubbed by the AAU because of a television contract hassle, and had then been reinstated when the issue was resolved. But in the meantime many of the athletes had made other plans and the AAU had to scramble at the eleventh hour to find enough athletes to send to the Soviet Union and then to Czechoslovakia for a meet there. Sam Bell reminded the AAU of the availability of Steve Heidenreich if the AAU was interested.

Heidi was aware of the sweet smell of ferns as he walked hurriedly into the business school building for a marketing class, his notebook in hand.

The instructor was ready to begin. Heidenreich wheeled to a seat in the classroom and did a double-take.

Was she staring at him?

He looked deeply into the blue eyes of a bubbly, trim brunette who was in the seat behind him. He smiled wryly, and she returned the smile.

"Hi."

The timbre of his voice pleased her.

"Hi." The class began and they turned away from each other.

For the remainder of the week they exchanged furtive glances and a few sentences and that, really, was all. It wasn't until some days later that Steve Heidenreich, Watertown, South Dakota, Beta Theta Pi, business major, formally met Beth Burnside, Kendallville, Indiana, Kappa Kappa Gamma, business major.

Their relationship began slowly and grew steadily, from chance meetings at the library to a tennis date to an invitation to a very special celebration party.

Heidenreich had worked out on a Monday afternoon and at 5 P.M., tired and sweaty, he arrived at his apartment and found a note from one of his roommates tacked to the door.

> Congrats buddy!
> You've been selected for the U.S. team. Some guy from the AAU called. You're supposed to be in New York tomorrow. The first meet is in Russia. Bet the vodka there is super. Let me know about the girls. I hear they all look like shot-putters and pachyderms.

Heidi called Beth and asked her to come to his apartment for a party that night. It was a mellow evening and Steve and Beth talked until almost midnight, getting to know each other better. When the party ended, Beth was ambivalent. She was happy that Steve had been chosen to run abroad but she wondered if he would bother to ever call her again. She certainly wanted him to. Steve took her to the Kappa Kappa Gamma house and they said goodbye.

Heidi returned to his apartment, finished packing, and grabbed a few fitful hours of sleep. The next morning he went to Indianapolis and from there he flew to New York, where it took three days to process his passport because he did not have his birth certificate with him.

On to Cologne, Germany, and then to Berlin. Heidenreich and the others in the United States group were taken by bus through the Wall into East Berlin. There, the Americans were made to stew at an East German airport, held up with red tape. Officials needed two hours to identify passports; there were not enough seats for them on the airplane. When Heidi finally landed at Kiev in a Soviet aircraft he had been traveling for fourteen hours.

Popejoy was waiting in the hotel lobby when Heidenreich arrived at 1:00 A.M. Heidi was exhausted. They had been assigned a hotel that could only be described as the pits: insects everywhere; mold on the soap; dried hair in the shower; and an inch of silt in the bottom of the bottled water.

Heidenreich and Popejoy, the U.S. entrants in the 1,500, were to run at noon. Heidi, sleeping in, missed breakfast but ate an early lunch with Popejoy and they discussed strategy but were careful not to reveal all their plans to each other.

Heidi walked out onto the track and sniffed the damp, chilly air. He was wearing warmup sweats with USA emblazoned on the back. For him this was a dream come true. He was now an international-class runner. He felt very American, and very proud.

There was a fine mist falling when Heidi, Popejoy and three Russians stepped to the line for the starter's gun. Crack. The tempo was slow and Popejoy thought to himself that he and Heidi could finish first and second in this race; the Russians were not kickers.

On the backstretch of the last lap Heidenreich sprinted. He quickly opened up a lead of twenty yards. Memories of the AAU race in Eugene and Heidi's wild, explosive sprint flashed through Popejoy's mind. "I wanted to reach out and grab him and tell him not to do that again," said Popejoy afterward. "He was too tired from the long trip." Too late. Heidi was gone, the impassioned effects of adrenalin having stirred the embers. "I didn't catch him until the final straightaway," said Popejoy.

Popejoy hit the tape first and looked around. Heidenreich was four or five steps behind, wobbly steps though they were. A Russian, throwing elbows everywhere, had muscled into second place but he was running as an unofficial entry in the 1,500-meter race so officially Heidi was second. His time was 3:43.6. Popejoy and Heidenreich hung on each other for a few moments and then, in the true spirit of détente, they joined hands with the Russian runners.

Heidi, though, was in a huff. He was angry that he had allowed the Russian to slip in ahead of him.

"You did super," Popejoy said to him. "I only wish that, for me and for yourself, you had held your kick just a little bit longer."

Heidi nodded. That night he slept like a baby. The next day he and Popejoy turned tourists, joining up with a Russian teenager who spoke English and wanted to buy a pair of their jeans and tagged along with the two Americans as they walked the streets of Kiev. Heidenreich stopped and watched old women who swept already clean streets with brooms, and searched several shops in vain for deodorant and aftershave. Their own had mysteriously disappeared from their rooms. In another store Heidi and Popejoy stood before a mirror and fitted themselves with shapkas, large fur caps. Other shoppers giggled and pointed. The two American athletes had tried on women's hats.

As soon as the American team landed in Prague, Popejoy and Heidi put their heads together and decided to hold their kicks. European runners often set a sizzling pace from the start but even Popejoy and Heidi were astonished at the whirlwind, suicidal sprint in which they found themselves when the 1,500 field broke from the starting line. They looked at each other in dismay; it was the fastest 110 yards Popejoy had run in a race. Were their chances gone? Heidenreich and Popejoy dropped back and cooled it until the bell sounded for the final 400 meters. Going into the final turn, Popejoy flew to the front and Heidi went, too, a step behind. Looking over his shoulder Popejoy saw Heidi's rakish sprint about to overtake him. But Heidenreich had squandered his energy. "In the last twenty yards, when he got tired, his arms would stiffen," said Popejoy later. "I saw his arms go and I thought, 'I'm going to win this thing.'"

He did. A Czech caught Heidi at the tape when he eased up, a dumb thing that Sam Bell had once blistered him for doing. The sting of defeat eased for Heidi when he learned his time, 3:38.8, a lifetime best. Popejoy's 3:38.4 equaled his own personal record.

The American team flew to Moscow for a layover en route to

the United States, arriving at 7 P.M. with several hours for sight-
seeing. They were enthralled at the majesty of Red Square
shrouded in fog. At 6 A.M. they were at the airport, their eyelids
heavy, boarding a plane for the flight home.

Heidenreich was jubilant and on a continual high. He had
tasted international racing and had done well. "I had achieved
what I had always wanted to do," he said later. "I had finally
made it and I said to myself, 'Man, you're only twenty-one and
you've got years of this left. Life is going to be great! Life is going
to be great . . . !'"

As soon as he arrived in Bloomington Heidi phoned Beth. She
wrote in her journal of the evening later that night:

> Even though he had just flown in, Steve asked Carla and me
> to go out with Ben and him. We went to the Time Out and
> danced. Poor Steve was practically sleepwalking but we still
> had a super time. The room was pulsating with the sounds of
> Paul McCartney and Wings and the song "Venus and Mars."
> As we danced, Steve put his arms tightly around me and, lean-
> ing down with his lips against my neck, he exclaimed: "You're
> so *tiny*!" Then he kissed me. I felt so small and helpless, com-
> pletely in his power. When he kissed me I melted right into
> the dance floor. He had me—I was his. The next day he came
> over to study with me. Concentration came only after a strug-
> gle with the temptation to gaze at him. Sometimes his elbow
> would touch mine and even Karen in the living room could
> probably have heard my heart beat. That week we saw each
> other every day and in two classes and studied together at
> noon and at night several times. On Saturday I had a birthday
> party for Vince. It was a super success and after we had
> champagne at midnight. Steve and I walked outside. We talked
> for a while. Then he gave me a real kiss! The one on the
> dance floor a week before had been a light, gay one but this
> one was very romantic. Then he said, "I've been waiting for
> four weeks to do that." We kissed some more. I've never
> been happier than I was then.

Meanwhile, Steve packed his Nike spikes and his warmups—
with USA emblazoned on the back—and flew to Cleveland for

the United States-Pan Africa meet at Baldwin Wallace College in suburban Berea.

Oh, did he run! Also in the mile event were Wilson Waigwa, the Kenyan, and Dick Buerkle, who in 1978 would set a world indoor mile record of 3:54.9.

For three laps Heidenreich was content to sit on the shoulders of the other two. He was a bundle of nerves but he watched the legs of those in front of him, judging the pace. He was running strongly, swiftly, and evenly and he believed in himself. "We were just starting the last lap and we were beginning to move pretty quick," remarked Heidi later, letting the race unfold in his memory. "I just sat tight. I had learned something about racing against Popejoy. I said to myself, 'Don't go too early.' So I sat and sat and sat."

The field was strung out now. Buerkle, Waigwa, and Heidi were comfortably in front, waging their own war. Down the backstretch they whizzed, each wondering what the other was thinking and planning.

Heidi's strategy going into the last curve was to sprint all the way in. He kicked, with absolutely no effort.

Heidenreich did not look around. He picked up his knees—he was lifting—and his arms seemed to reach higher and higher, uppercutting furiously. He sailed into the homestretch and actually felt as if he were floating. How easy this was! No strain and he was flying with effortless rhythm. Waigwa and Buerkle hung on for as long as they could and then they broke and let go. Heidenreich's legs devoured the track and he snapped the tape, raising both arms in a salute. His time was 3:58.4. Waigwa was next in 3:59.5 and Buerkle third in 4:00.6.

Steve and Beth had been together constantly, studying at night, bicycling in the afternoons or going for long walks. This was the first real romance for each of them. They depended on each other for support. To Beth, Steve was wise and understanding. To Steve, Beth was sophisticated, chic, and tender.

Steve went to Eugene, Oregon, again, this time for the trials that would determine the American team for the 1975 Pan

American Games to be held during the next month, October, at Mexico City.

The runners in the 1,500 at Eugene all seemed reluctant to take the lead until Tony Waldrop, once a sensation at the University of North Carolina, zoomed to the front. Heidi and Scott Daggatt of the University of Oregon also put the hammer down. "I wanted first place," says Heidenreich. "I was really greedy. I wanted to win it. I should have cooled my jets and been satisfied with second place because the first two placers made the U.S. team. I tried to pass Waldrop with 300 meters left and he fought me around the whole last curve and wouldn't let me pass him. When we got into the homestretch he had a ten-yard lead on me and I was in the second lane."

Staying there opened a spot on the inside for Daggatt, who in lane one ran past Heidi and took the Number two place on the team from him. Waldrop ran 3:50.5, Daggatt 3:51.1, and Heidi 3:51.4. Later, Heidi assuaged his bruised ego by quaffing pitchers of beer with Ken Popejoy and two other Indiana runners, Tom Burleson and Pat Mandera, all of whom had failed to make the team. The discussion centered around the question of whether Heidenreich should have stayed in lane two or moved over into lane one and forced Daggatt to go to the outside. That, had Heidi done it, probably would have saved his position on the team.

Beth and her mother met Steve at the airport in Fort Wayne, Indiana, which was only a few miles from Kendallville. Beth wrote later:

> He'd gotten third and he was very disappointed because he didn't qualify to go to Mexico City. Still, that summer was the best I ever had. We never fought and the times we spent together we were continually happy. We both said, "Can this last?" Everything was perfect. He was running well, we both had done well in summer school classes, and we had each other.
>
> We kept saying something was going to happen. Little did we know. I loved to watch him run; he is just like a deer when he runs. Graceful. Anyone who would put that much time in on running amazed me. I could not identify with that dedication to running in any way. Runners seem to be built lean but not necessarily tall.

Their personalities are the same. They are fiery, the inner part you don't see, and outwardly they appear mellow and reserved.

Steve returned to Bloomington early in that September of 1975 from Rome, where he had finished second in the 1,500 at the World University Games behind West Germany's Thomas Wessinghage, who had run 3:39.73. Heidi's time was 3:40.56.

Beth and Steve did not see as much of each other because both were busy. They began to fight over the people Beth called his "cronies" at the Beta house, where he was living. During that summer he had been in an apartment with two phantom roommates who were never around, and so they had privacy—Beth had no competition for his time. That autumn, Beth felt she had become expendable. She was hurt and tried to be graceful but she nagged him, and he in turn became angry. He said the fights were her fault for nagging; she said they were his fault for being thoughtless. "I really think it was because we didn't understand or accept each other's needs," she said later.

The Big Ten Conference had granted Heidenreich an extra season of cross-country eligibility in 1975 for the 1973 season when he had been red-shirted because of an injury. He also had been granted extra eligibility for the indoor season in 1976 for the season he missed as a sophomore because of injuries. But all this was not accomplished without some initial opposition from other Big Ten coaches who, as a discomfited Sam Bell has put it, "saw someone getting what they thought was an advantage. It was small of them."

Heidenreich's final cross-country season at IU was not impressive, probably because his training and racing during the summer months had been aimed at sharpness for the 1,500 and mile, and not for the long distances required in cross-country training.

He was defeated in three successive meets at the tail end of the season by Craig Virgin, a gutsy farm boy from Lebanon, Illinois, who was building a phenomenal cross-country record at the University of Illinois, and who became the first to win the Big Ten cross-country title four straight years. Virgin, the greatest distance runner in Big Ten history, made the United States Olympic team in 1976, finishing second behind Frank Shorter in the

10,000 meters at the Olympic Trials in Eugene. Virgin, strong of spirit and as courageous a runner as Heidi, won the NCAA cross-country championship in that autumn of 1975 on a course at Penn State University. Two and a half minutes after Virgin, the winner, had sprinted into the chute, Steve Heidenreich straggled home in 195th place and shouted to all those near him, "You turkeys! Wait until indoor season and we'll see who's winning then!"

It was true. The good runs came later. For the moment, Heidi was grim and grumpy, determined to get tougher and stronger.

The next month, December, Steve moved out of the Beta house and into an apartment. Beth was delighted. She wrote:

Hurrah! It wasn't quite as ideal as it had been in the summer because his roommates were fixtures and privacy was rare. However, our relationship did improve 100 percent. Steve began taking important things more seriously. He was determined to pull a 4-point [a straight-A average] and he was headed in that direction. He was allocating more time my way, even though most of it was spent together at the library. He told me there were three things that were important to him. They were:

    (1) Running
    (2) A 4-point
    (3) Me

Still, I didn't feel pushed aside. Running cut into our time together but to be perfectly truthful I was more proud of his good grades than I was of his running. The fact that he can do both really impressed me. Things are really looking good. We have had more good times than bad. I don't have any idea what the future holds but I hope Steve and I are able to stay together because I love him dearly.

Sunday, January 25, 1976, was a lazy day in Bloomington. Steve Heidenreich had celebrated his four-minute mile at the Indiana University indoor track the previous afternoon by dancing to the throb of the Saturday night fever. He was zonked out and fast asleep. His race had been a record-breaker. He had become the first in the history of the Big Ten Conference to run the distance that fast indoors. Afterward, Sam Bell was surrounded by newsmen who asked what he had in mind for his world-class miler. "He wanted to go to another indoor meet next week but I told him no," commented the coach. "There are a lot of meets coming up and I don't want him to get too tired. I want to make sure he's got something left in June when the Olympic Trials come around."

The Olympic Games, that quadrennial event of athletic jousting among the world's nations—all in the spirit of fostering peace and fellowship, of course—would be at Montreal in July. Already, spiraling inflation was pushing the cost of the Games to unheard-of levels.

Already, the word was out that security would be impenetrable at Montreal. For anyone who had lived through those horrifying days at Munich in 1972, the outrage could not have been greater or the grief deeper. The Games there had been meant to erase memories of German militarism and yet, as in a nightmare, Jewish blood had been shed again when the Black September terrorist group murdered eleven members of the Israeli team.

Some superstitious athletes never talk openly of their hopes or dreams for a place on an Olympic team, fearing that to do so will bring them bad luck. Heidenreich, however, was not afraid of contemplating the possibility. In one of his favorite fantasies he placed himself in the 1,500-meter final at Montreal with New Zealand's John Walker and Tanzania's Filbert Bayi. Heidi's chances of making the United States Olympic team appeared to be completely credible and whenever anyone asked him what he thought about this, he answered, "Well, things are going pretty good, you know, and if I can just keep it up and keep things going I might be on that team."

Heidenreich's confidence had recently been shaken, though. At the Big Ten indoor meet at the University of Wisconsin in Madison in early March he was disqualified in the 1,000 when judges ruled that he was guilty of interference. He and another runner jostled as Heidi attempted to pass. He also was disqualified in the mile when he false-started. On the bus trip back to Bloomington Steve Weiss wrote Heidi a note and passed it back to him. Heidi read:

What's going on with your mind? Track is an aggressive sport but you are *too* aggressive and if you do that in Eugene [site of the Olympic trials] or in Montreal the result will be the same. They'll throw you out. Cool it, Heidi.

Because Heidenreich had not been among the first three in the mile at the Big Ten meet, Indiana had to appeal for his certification to enter the NCAA indoor championships at Detroit even though his 4:00.0 mile was the fourth fastest nationally among collegians in that 1976 indoor season.

Word did not come to Sam Bell until Wednesday in the week of the NCAA meet from the conference that Heidi could run at Detroit's Cobo Hall on that Friday. Heidenreich, anxious and upset, was not in the proper psychological frame of mind to run well. On March 12 in the preliminaries he clocked a slow 4:-15.10 and was sixth in his heat, failing to advance to the final. He really did not know what happened. "I was leading and in control of the race with two laps to go," he said later, "and all of a sudden on a curve I was off the board track and running on concrete. Five people crowded ahead of me and I went from first to last in the space of ten feet."

Beth Burnside and her mother had driven to Detroit to watch Heidi run. When he did not make the final all three piled into the car and drove to Kendallville, where Beth and Steve stayed at the Burnside home until Sunday morning. On Sunday, March 14, the two returned to Bloomington by bus and Steve studied the entire trip. He had an "A" average in all of his courses, from history to investment to advanced finance, and he had vowed that he would settle for nothing less than a 4-point, hadn't he?

His race at Cobo Hall had left him in a state of inner turmoil. On both Monday and Tuesday he had run hard in afternoon workouts, exorcising the frustration from his system. On that ill-fated Tuesday night, March 16, after studying at the library with Beth, he was itchy to get in his five-mile run on the snowy roads. His combativeness was showing. And that night the results were tragic: His entire world turned over.

7

That Wednesday, March 17, policeman Randy Harper looked at his watch. It was 12:05 A.M., about twenty-five minutes after Steve Heidenreich had been hit on Kinser Pike.

As soon as Harper had answered the request of the Bloomington Police Department dispatcher that an assisting patrol car go to the accident site and he was en route, he began mentally clicking off the possibilities. "I'd been told it was a runner and I didn't exactly know who but I had to wonder because you'd see this Heidenreich all around. I'd seen him run out in that area often," he later said.

When Mike Dutchman, Steve's other roommate, returned to the apartment early that morning, he and Mark Schlundt went immediately to Bloomington Hospital, arriving about 1:30 A.M. They could hear Heidenreich's moans in the examining room, a haunting sound repeated over and over. Sam Bell, his voice quivering, informed them that the prognosis was bad.

Schlundt noticed that Heidi's running clothes had been assembled in an eerie fashion on the floor in a hallway, as if he were wearing them. John Gaston, a Bloomington policeman who was moonlighting in the emergency room, laid the clothes out while he inspected them. The sweat bottoms were dark blue with red and white stripes, part of the USA uniform. The left knee was torn and the seat was scuffed. Schlundt pointed out the rip to Dutch-

76

man and muttered, "Heidi will be pissed." His red nylon rain jacket was bloodstained. The right shoulder and the right elbow were torn.

When Heidenreich was brought to the emergency room and Dr. Rak was finished with his preliminary examination, he listed him in a grade III coma. This meant that Heidi was responding to painful stimulation by trying to withdraw from stimulus or to push it away from him.

In a head injury of the type Heidenreich suffered, the crucial question is the condition of the brain, not the skull. Fractures of the skull are in themselves of little importance unless they are pressing on the brain. A blow of sufficient force to the head will in all likelihood cripple delicate brain centers. The brain, similar to a bowl of jelly encased in the hard, bony skull for protection, is constantly in fluid motion. Before Heidenreich was moved to the operating room Dr. Rak looked carefully for neurological signs produced by pinching and stimulating certain parts of the body, for Heidi's reaction to these were the doctor's preliminary semaphores of the severity of the damage.

The cerebral angiogram detected that at least one blood vessel had been ruptured. The doctor diagnosed a hematoma—a hemorrhage which is an injury of extreme surgical emergency. The doctor feared at first that the hematoma might be subdural, meaning that it could be building deep within the brain.

The fracture was comminuted—broken into multiple fragments—and it extended into the middle fossa, an indentation at the base of the skull.

Heidenreich's brain had begun to swell following impact in the accident. Dr. Rak injected him with mannitol, an osmotic dehydrating agent that removes fluid from the brain, just before the surgery. The rigid cranial bones left little room for the engorgement of blood flowing from the broken vein, the cerebrospinal fluid, and the brain tissue itself. An increase in the volume of any one of these takes place at the expense of the other two and creates pressure which interferes with the proper functioning of nerve cells. It is very much like pumping air into a tire: There is only so much room and so much air that can be pumped in before the saturation point is reached.

At 5:12 A.M. the anesthesiologists started the sodium pentothal that put Heidi into a deep sleep. A mask was placed over his face and oxygen administered.

Succinylcholine, a muscle relaxant, stilled his body. An endo-tracheal tube was inserted into his throat. His shaved head was scrubbed and disinfected and placed in a foam rubber donut that inhibited movement. His eyes were taped shut.

With a scalpel, Dr. Rak scratched out a superficial line on the scalp in a U shape on the right side of Heidi's head extending behind the ear. The line served as a marking. Green sterile towels were clamped into place on Heidi's head. The rest of his body was draped with green sheets. A nurse turned his head to the left.

At 5:55 A.M. the doctor began the surgery, a craniotomy. He deepened the slash on the scalp by following the line he had marked. He peeled back the scalp from the underlying muscle. With a nitrogen-driven drill he made four burr holes in a box formation, each about one-half inch in diameter. As he did, fluid spurted. He sawed the skull, connecting the four holes. A rangeur, a pliers-type instrument, enabled him to bite the bone out.

The brain lay bare. The doctor found an epidural hematoma, an accumulation of blood in the epidural space between the skull and the dura mater, a membrane that is the outer covering of the brain. The dura was torn and so was the brain tissue under it, the lesion being in the temporal lobe. Dr. Rak removed the large clot and tied off a ruptured cortical vein on the surface of the brain, quieting the blood spasms.

Two hours and twenty-five minutes after he began, Dr. Rak finished the surgery. A few moments later he called Watertown and explained to DeLoris Heidenreich what he had done.

"Stephen's brain was ripped," the doctor told her, "which indicates to me that it was really slammed around. I took the bone from the skull out and left it out and sewed the muscle that's over the surface of the skull to the dura so that everything is sealed. There is enough room for the brain to swell through the bone opening. This will lower the pressure and this is what we're hoping for; that the pressure will lower enough so that he will survive.

"I would like you and your husband to come to Bloomington today. Can you do that?"

"Yes, of course," she said anxiously. "We'll be there later this afternoon."

"Good. I'll see you then."

Those early hours of the morning had been excruciating for DeLoris and Merle Heidenreich. After the original call had come DeLoris had washed clothes, just to give herself something to do, and then she went back to bed. Merle could not sleep. He paced the living room floor, walking from window to window, sad and afraid. As he paced the words from Psalm 121 glided across his mind, words that he had read often when he was deep in the bunkers in Korea.

He will not let your foot be moved,
He who keeps you will not slumber.
Behold, he who keeps Israel
Will neither slumber nor sleep.

The Lord will keep you from all evil
He will keep your life.
The Lord will keep your going out and your coming in
From this time forth and for evermore.

At Bloomington Hospital, the early morning hours seemed to pass in slow motion. While Sam Bell waited, a phone call from the Bloomington Police Department came for Officer Gaston. Bell could overhear parts of the conversation, enough to piece together the information that someone had come to the station and told the police he thought he had hit something on Kinser Pike.

That was, in fact, exactly what had happened. At 3:00 A.M., Sonny Andrew Thorsrud, a 19-year-old senior at a Bloomington high school, walked into the station accompanied by his father and his uncle.

Officers Becky Holder and Todd McCormick took a statement from the youth and read him his rights. He waived them, and

Holder then asked him to describe his actions "late on the evening of March 16, 1976."

Sonny Thorsrud cleared his throat. "All I can say is I was traveling north on Kinser Pike and I didn't know there was anything alongside of the road or anything like that," he said. "I felt a bump as if I had hit something and I guess I didn't stop. I just kept on going and went home."

"And what did you do once you got there?" asked Holder.

"I went to bed and I thought about two minutes or so and I woke up my dad and talked to him. I said I didn't know if it was a dog or maybe if it could have been worse—like a person. We decided to come down here and see what—if I had hit anybody, any person."

"When you struck whatever it was, did you apply your brakes?" asked McCormick.

"Yes, I did. And then I looked in the rear view mirror. I didn't see anything and I don't know, I just kept thinking like maybe it was a dog or cat. I didn't see any reason to stop or anything like that; I guess I should have but I just kept on going towards home," said Thorsrud.

The questioning continued.

HOLDER: "Was anyone else in the car with you?"

THORSRUD: "No. Just me."

HOLDER: "Are you under any medication for anything?"

THORSRUD: "No, ma'am."

HOLDER: "Were you under the influence of anything this evening?"

THORSRUD: "No, ma'am."

HOLDER: "Narcotics or alcohol?"

THORSRUD: "No, ma'am."

McCORMICK: "Had you been drinking this evening?"

THORSRUD: "No, sir."

Becky Holder looked at Todd McCormick. As she would file in her report later, she said that it was evident to both officers that they could smell liquor in the room. At 3:24 A.M. McCormick administered a breathalyzer examination to Thorsrud, who tested .097 percent. Under Indiana law .10 is considered drunk.

When the result of the test was read to Thorsrud, he admitted that, yes, he had one beer during the evening. And even when McCormick explained to him that the chemical reading of the test showed that he had much more than one beer to drink, Thorsrud stuck to his original statement.

Holder's report said that William Thorsrud first told the police that his son had awakened him at 1:00 A.M., but later said he thought it was more like midnight and that his son had said he had arrived home at about 11:30.

Sonny Thorsrud agreed to take a polygraph test but his father discouraged him from doing so, explaining to him that an attorney should be consulted first.

At 6:30 that morning, Wednesday the 17th, the phone rang in the dormitory room of Linda Heidenreich and Nancy Lynne at Augustana College in Sioux Falls, South Dakota. Nancy answered.

"It's your mom," she yelled to Linda, who was bathing. That's odd, Linda said to herself. Why should she be calling? During the previous weekend DeLoris Heidenreich had been on the campus for a mother-daughter fête and on that Friday, the 12th, Linda and David Nerdig, a theological student, had become engaged, so she and her parents had been in touch quite recently. Linda took the receiver from Nancy.

"Linda, I have some bad news," she heard her mother say. "I want you to sit down and then as soon as we're done talking I want you to call Dave and have him come right over."

Linda inhaled sharply.

"Steve was out running and he was run over. He's in the hospital and it doesn't look good—his head was badly hurt. We're waiting to hear from the doctors. They called us after midnight to get permission to operate. We will probably go there today."

". . . Is it bad, Mom?"

"Yes, I think it is. I'll call you back when I hear from the hospital."

Linda began to cry. The tears quickly were flooding down her face. She was conscious of trying to scream but could not. The room and Nancy blurred into one floating image.

"Do you want me to call Dave?," asked Nancy. Linda nodded and Nancy dialed.

"Dave, this is Nancy Lynne," she said when he answered. "You better get over here right away. . . . It's Linda's brother. She needs you."

David Nerdig could barely hear Nancy's voice, so penetrating were Linda's cries. "It sent shivers through me," he said, recalling it.

Soon, doors began opening on the floor where Linda Heidenreich lived, and girls huddled in the hallway, horrified by the shrieking they heard. Linda, sitting on a bed, cried harder. Nancy came to her and cuddled her in her arms, rocking her.

"Jesus . . . help us," said Nancy Lynne, softly.

Ten minutes later David Nerdig arrived from his dormitory at the south end of the campus.

"What happened?" he asked.

"I don't know," replied Linda.

The phone rang. It was Linda's mother again. She filled him in on the details of the hit-and-run incident and as they were talking, Linda grabbed the phone.

". . . Mom, I don't want Steve to die."

"Nobody does," said her mother, who then instructed firmly, "Now you get hold of yourself." She took a deep breath and calmed herself down. The sound of her mother's voice, so steady and reassuring despite her own emotional upheaval, made Linda feel guilty for carrying on. What was important was her brother and the family.

At eight o'clock that morning, Beth Burnside was returning to her room at the Kappa Kappa Gamma house in Bloomington from breakfast when she heard the phone ringing. Once . . . twice . . . three times. If it was Steve she had a long list of grievances to relate to him, starting with the 2:30 A.M. call that he was supposed to have made with a report on the term paper.

It was Sam Bell. The instant she heard the coach's voice she realized something was wrong. Summoning a bravado she didn't feel, she listened.

"Beth, Heidi's been hit by a car and I'm here at the hospital," said Bell. "There is no point in your coming here now. He has had surgery and he won't wake up until this afternoon. He's been seriously hurt. All the damage was to his head but the doctor hopes he will live . . ."

For the first time in her life Beth lost complete control of herself. The coach's words echoed, hammered at her, seeming to ricochet off the walls. She felt as if her insides were coming out. With gut-wrenching cries she hurled herself, belly-first, against a sofa.

Again. Again. Again.

"N-o-o . . . !

"No . . . !

"Steeeeeevvvvvve!"

She was surrounded immediately by others in the sorority house who attempted to console and comfort her. She did not even hear what they were saying. A hollow, sick sensation had washed over her. All that screaming had left her empty. She thought, somebody tell me this isn't happening. Tears were streaming down her cheeks. But within an hour she had managed to displace and settle her fears.

In that hour of trauma she suddenly was sure that Steve would live, that he would be mentally whole again, that he would run again. She had absolutely no doubt and her inner assuredness gave her a strange peace. This was to be a tranquility that provided a shield and steadied her in the tumultous days ahead. Her attitude amazed those about her. They asked often how she could be so positive, so sure? She didn't know, but she was.

At almost the same moment that Beth Burnside had been on the phone with Sam Bell, Steve's younger brother, Roger, was sitting down for a final exam in calculus at Northwestern University in Evanston, Illinois. Roger had been cramming and had stayed up until four o'clock studying.

When he put down his pencil and handed the exam to the

instructor he felt drained. He went straight to his apartment, planning to take a bath and go to bed. On the door was a note with the name of John Pont, Northwestern athletic director, printed at the top. It said: "Please call Sam Bell in Bloomington."

Roger Heidenreich's telephone was out of order and no one had been able to get in touch with him. Bell, frustrated when he could not reach Roger, had called Pont's office and asked for help.

From another apartment, Roger dialed Bell's number and he, too, had difficulty comprehending the coach's staggering news, not wanting to believe the words he was hearing.

"Roger, Steve's been in a bad accident," said Bell.

Steve's been in an accident?

"All of the damage was to his head. I was at the hospital all night with him. The doctor is more hopeful than when he began the operation."

An accident? Roger stared at the receiver in his hand.

A thousand questions rushed through his head. What was he supposed to do? How would his parents reach him? Should he go home, go to Bloomington, or stay where he was? God, he needed to talk to someone.

He knocked on the door of the next apartment, walked in and stammered: "I've got to talk to you guys." Then he burst into tears, telling them, "My brother got hurt in an accident and he's really bad. And he might die." The occupants of the apartment looked at him wordlessly. Roger sat for fifteen minutes trying to get himself together as they attempted to comfort him.

He then returned to his apartment and, on an impulse, picked up the phone and it was working. He started to call his sister Linda in Sioux Falls. What was her number? God, he could not remember it. He dialed what he thought was directory assistance at Augustana College.

"I'd like the number for Linda Heidenreich," said Roger.

There were a few seconds of silence at the other end.

"This is her place," Roger heard the voice say, finally. He had dialed his sister's number and did not know it. In his shock his finger had worked automatically.

ABOVE: Steve Heidenreich, high school sophomore, on his last leg of the ESD Cross Country Meet in 1968.

RIGHT: Steve wins the Anchor Sprint medley at Watertown, 1971. *Photo by Bill Tredway.*

Watertown High Cross Country team, 1968. Steve is in front row, far left. *Photo by Ron Lenz.*

Training on the Watertown track in 1971, Steve passes Jeff Schemmel. *Photo by Ron Lenz.*

LEFT: Training at Indiana University, fall of 1972.
RIGHT: The finish of Steve's first winning race at IU with a time of 4:00. *Photo by Dave Parker.*

Steve wins a mile run at an IU indoor track meet, February 1976.
Photo by Phil Whitlow.

Heidi trains with Bruce Jenner.

Steve's last race before the accident, an NCAA meet, March 1976. *Photo by Neil I. Cohen.*

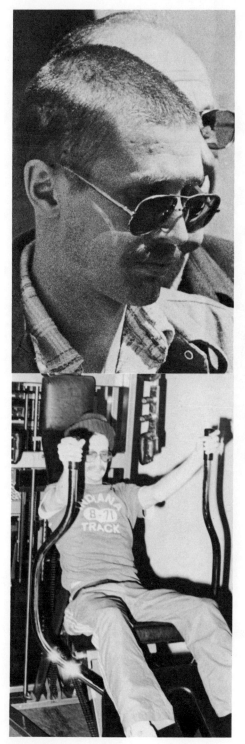

Steve comes home from the hospital.

The painful road back: Steve, still wearing the cap to protect his skull, lifting weights at the D.C. Health Center, Watertown, summer 1976. *Photo by J. T. Fey.*

Heidi, back in practice. *Photo © Dave Repp.*

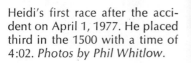

Heidi's first race after the accident on April 1, 1977. He placed third in the 1500 with a time of 4:02. *Photos by Phil Whitlow*.

Photo by D. Bunde.

Heidi and Connie Gingery, his fiancée.

"Roger, is that you? This is Nancy Lynne, Linda's roommate. Roger, are you all right?"

"No . . . no, I'm not."

Linda was not there but Roger had made his decision by the time he got off the phone. He would go to Bloomington. He called Allegheny Airlines and booked a flight that night.

In Bloomington, there was dismay as word of Steve Heidenreich was flashed throughout the campus on Wednesday morning. The entire town had been totally and awfully shattered.

Heidenreich's teammates reacted with disbelief. Dean Reinke had always questioned the propriety of running at night, and the stretch of Kinser Pike where Heidi was struck was dimly lit— everyone knew that. "Dammit, he shouldn't have been out there," Reinke said at the time. "It finally caught up with him."

Dan Visscher, who idolized Heidenreich, took a philosophic view. "He wasn't really human, you know, with the inner strength that he possessed," says Visscher. "In a way it's like somebody would look on a thoroughbred horse whose leg had been broken. It was kind of like he was so high and so far above everything that somebody had to shoot him down." In the days that followed, Visscher during his training runs had visions of Heidenreich's twisted, crumpled body lying in the road. Hallucinatory images in a blurry outline.

When Steve Weiss heard that Heidi had been hit his thoughts drifted back to the note he had written to Heidenreich ten days earlier admonishing him for his aggressiveness. "I could picture, like, here was a car that was maybe pushing him off the road but he wasn't going to give an inch . . . he was going to play chicken with the car," says Weiss, whose running diary for March 17 read this way:

> Heidenreich meets with Steve Prefontaine syndrome. In hospital, critical condition, head injuries. Everyone really pissed because he got run over by a car. Man, it sure is a dark day. Do it for Heidi.

Mike Durkin found out when he saw a picture of Heidenreich in the Chicago *Tribune*. Then his eyes were drawn to a headline and the story. He, too, stared in disbelief.

Jeff Schemmel read of the accident in the Topeka *Capital-Journal* and he phoned Sam Bell. The call was one of hundreds that Bell received in the next forty-eight hours from people across the nation. The switchboard at Bloomington Hospital, as well, was extraordinarily busy on this Wednesday, recording 157 calls inquiring about the condition of Steve Heidenreich.

Heidi was taken to the recovery room at 8:30 A.M. in very critical condition and transferred to the intensive care unit an hour later. For the next thirty-six hours he flirted with death. He was in a coma for the next eight days.

Heidenreich's neurological status was determined by the responses he made when the nurses examined him, pinching his nipples, applying pressure to his fingertips or squeezing the trapezius muscles between his neck and shoulder. They looked for those ominous signs that indicated abnormal changes in his condition. Recognition and treatment could halt any further deterioration before irreversible damage developed. The intensive-care nurses noted that his color and his breathing were good and that his pupils were equal and reactive only an hour after the operation. It was encouraging, for it meant that his brain had not slipped across and was not compressing the brain stem.

Heidi had become decerebrate before and after surgery—his limbs were rigidly extended and his arms hyperpronated. This condition indicated to Dr. Rak that the brain stem was not functioning. Impulses were not being transmitted by the network of cells and fibers in the brain stem to the cerebral cortex and upper part of the brain, keeping it in an alert state. Because of this the doctor knew Heidenreich was on the borderline of serious permanent brain damage.

Later that Wednesday, a driver from the IU athletic department took Beth and Bell to Indianapolis to meet Merle and DeLoris Heidenreich, who had taken a connecting flight from Minneapolis. Steve's parents had left Watertown barely able to talk, communicating the vital things to one another in silence. Sitting stiffly on the plane they were, together, running the same questions over and over in their minds and searching for answers.

Why?

Why Steve?

Their faith in God was being tested. Was there a meaning? How could they just pick up the pieces and continue on as before?

At 4:30 P.M. the Heidenreichs, weary and drawn, stepped into the hushed hospital room, suppressing their emotions, bound together by the danger their son faced. Merle was shaken by the chilling sight of his son in the bed. He could not take his eyes off Steve's shaved head and his torso with tubes coming out of everywhere. As he looked he wondered sadly what his son could tell them about the accident at this moment if it was possible.

DeLoris was still hopeful. She knew her son well. "He has a long way to go," she said, "and yet he is alive. He is alive."

Dr. Rak took the parents into the corridor.

"What are his chances?" asked Merle.

"You must understand that each case is different," replied the doctor, "but the odds right now are low that he will survive with good results. It will be touch and go.

"By good results I mean doing what he was doing before. People injured like Stephen has been are rarely, if ever, exactly the same. That's a TV soap opera where people wake up from severe head injuries and in the next episode they're okay.

"In general, persons who have blood clots on the surface of the brain and who are decerebrate, which Stephen was, have a survival rate that is very low. It is probably five percent, even with surgery. If you operate and you have only a five percent survival rate, the majority of those patients are vegetative. Rarely do these patients recover and, for example, do what Stephen was doing. I mean, go on and finish college. We could *not* expect him to compete again as a runner."

The actual damage, the tear to Heidenreich's temporal lobe, was small but it affected many parts of his brain. For one lobe to function correctly, cooperation is necessary among all the lobes, the temporal, occipital, parietal, and frontal.

The doctor in the days ahead paid close attention to the movements of Heidi's limbs on both sides of his body, since many skills and sights and sounds are crossed, interacted, and processed on the opposite side of the brain.

So that was it; Heidi had a minimal chance. And if he made it, how far back could he come? Could he be capable of anything resembling a normal life?

On Woodbluff Court, Sam Bell had just fallen off to sleep, although it was only 6:00 P.M. He had seen his team off to Tuscaloosa and had been up almost seventeen hours and was wrung out emotionally by the monstrous events of the day.

He had been asleep only a short while when the ringing of the telephone woke him. What he heard cleared his fogginess. The voice at the other end said, "This is William Thorsrud—I'm Sonny Thorsrud's father. I want you to know we are praying for Steve . . .''

Sam Bell's heart jumped to his throat.

"My God," he said in recounting the call, "I was so relieved. I thought someone was calling me to tell me that Heidi had died!"

He couldn't go back to sleep but instead paced until it was time to meet Roger Heidenreich's flight, which touched down in Bloomington at 9:30 P.M. The two men just looked at each other, unable to exchange small talk.

The coach took Roger directly through the emergency room at the hospital and to the fifth floor. Roger seemed to sense death everywhere. The pungent, sterile odors of the hospital were offensive.

He stepped slowly into the room and stared at his brother. Steve's bandaged head seemed misshapen. He looked so *hurt*. And one of his legs was twitching! Roger's mouth felt dry. Surely this was an apparition. This wasn't the Steve he knew. The Steve who got first place in the races. The Steve he had stood and cheered, who was achieving and strong, sturdy and so full of life.

Roger shivered. He had to leave the room and Bell took him to the lobby. Seeing his parents, he broke into tears and ran to them. "You've got to be strong," his mother whispered as they hugged. "How can we get through this if you're not strong?"

The four walked to Bell's car in the hospital parking lot and he drove them to his home. He and his wife had insisted they stay with them as long as they had to. Before going to bed, Merle took out a brown, pocket-sized prayer book and handed it to Roger. "Here, son," he said, smiling faintly. "I used this in Korea when things were rough. It might help you tonight."

The Heidenreichs went upstairs. Before he shut off the lights and walked up the stairs himself, the coach caught a glimpse of the saying he had framed and hung in the downstairs hallway. It was a paraphrase of a verse from Corinthians and it read:

RUN THAT YOU MAY OBTAIN.

Not for medals. For the personal experiences and significance that running had come to mean and the athletes whose lives he had shared.

That's what he had obtained.

Images of Heidi surfaced.

Kiev.

Prague.

Kinser Pike.

Sam Bell wept.

8

The second day.

Thursday, March 18. Midnight. Little improvement. Steve Heidenreich's chart at this hour showed:

—Pupils equal and reactive to light; do not appear to focus. Grips blanket with both hands when stimulated. Moves all extremities when stimulated.

The family, including Beth, was permitted to be with Steve for five minutes each hour from 8:00 A.M. until 10:00 P.M. During that time one member would go to the room and assist in the stimulation. The immediate concern was to bring Heidi out of the coma. The nursing staff instructed the family how to squeeze a nipple, pinch the shoulder, shout close to his face and so on. Withdrawing from the pain and noise would be normal response. In fact, during his fifteen-day stay in the intensive care unit he kicked one nurse and punched another while he was being examined. This hostility is common among brain-damaged patients and is sometimes more a result of a patient being frustrated in his efforts to communicate than of being disoriented.

Thus began a solemn string of days of waiting and hoping. Days that blended together. Days when the slightest sign of improvement would produce instantaneous jubilation or, conversely,

90

when there was no improvement, deep depression.

Bloomington Hospital became home. DeLoris did needlepoint. Merle read. Roger walked and talked with others in the lobby on the main floor, a lobby bordered on one side by an abundance of green plants that was an attempt to give the room life and hope amid the sickness. Beth's mother joined her. She moved into the Ramada Inn and came to the hospital daily. While Heidi remained comatose, Beth attended no classes.

11:00 A.M. *Thursday.*

Roger's turn to go to the room. He could barely look at his brother. He recoiled at the sight. Heidi's jaw, snapped on both sides and not yet wired, hung askew. His skin appeared clammy. It had the ashen color of death, and Roger found it grotesque. He couldn't bring himself to touch his brother. Steve's eyes, when the nurses pushed back the eyelids, were blood red and the veins were prominent. Lying there he looked so thin, so shrunken, so hurt—so near death.

". . . Steve, this is Roger! I'm here! Steve, can you hear me?"

Gradually, Roger felt better about his daily chore of yelling in his brother's face. "I realized it was important that he knew I was there, even if he couldn't hear me . . . even if it wasn't going to matter," recalls Roger. "It was important to me, too. It gave me a feeling that I was contributing."

Roger returned to the waiting area. His father put down his magazine and looked up.

"Anything to report?"

Roger shook his head. The watch continued.

On this day, Dr. Rak talked privately with DeLoris and Merle, amplifying his candid remarks of the previous day and suggesting to the parents that they should begin considering the possibility of a life in a nursing home for their twenty-three-year-old son. Steve had celebrated his birthday exactly one month to the day before he had been struck down.

In fairness to the parents, the doctor felt he had to touch all bases, all possibilities. His mood was somber, but he had by no means given up. Later in the day he administered ten milligrams of Ritalin, a synthetic amphetamine that had been used with success on patients thought to be brain stem injured, and which could give the doctor a sneak preview of how Heidi might react. It was encouraging—Heidi became momentarily alert and he mumbled something, but he remained in a coma.

Richard Rak had been in Bloomington for only the past five and a half months. Before then, there had been no staff neurosurgeon at Bloomington Hospital. Patients with massive head injuries had been transferred to Methodist Hospital at Indianapolis, an hour and thirty minutes away. The medical community in Bloomington had not been eager to put out a welcome mat for any neurosurgeon. The hospital was jammed with patients already and physicians were vying for beds. But Richard Rak had quickly made his mark in the community.

Twenty-nine years old—exceptionally young to hold such a position—Rak had been graduated from high school at sixteen and entered medical school at Northwestern at nineteen. He happens to be a runner as well, and unless his sciatica flares, he puts in several miles daily. Had he not been in Bloomington when Steve was injured, the extra time it would have taken to transport Steve to Indianapolis could have meant irreversible damage or death.

On Thursday, Sam Bell phoned Tom Berry, a Bloomington attorney. "Steve might die," the coach said in a voice tight with anguish, "and if he doesn't he might be a vegetable. Stand by, Tom, and take whatever action is necessary. If he dies you'll handle his estate. If he's vegetative you'll represent his parents. If he survives I want you to represent him."

There were people praying for Heidi—by name—every day, in all parts of the country, and this was enormously reassuring to his parents. Prayer vigils were being held as far away as Los Angeles and Denver; in Bloomington; in Kenosha, Wisconsin; and in Sioux Falls, where a communion service was conducted at Augustana College.

A Lutheran minister, driving from St. Joseph, Missouri, to Cameron, Missouri, turned on his car radio and heard this national sports report on CBS:

. . . And tonight in Bloomington, Indiana, Steve Heidenreich, one of America's top collegiate milers, fights for his life. Heidenreich is the fastest miler in Indiana University history and was fourth in the NCAA outdoor meet at Provo, Utah, in June. He was struck by a car while he was running late Tuesday night in Bloomington . . .

The minister included Heidenreich in prayers at churches in St. Joseph and Cameron.

At Tuscaloosa, Alabama, Tom Burleson, a teammate of Heidi who was on the spring track trip, had just won the 1,500 in the meet that afternoon. He snapped on the TV in his motel room and heard:

. . . And after this message, more news on Indiana mile star Steve Heidenreich . . .

Burleson swallowed hard. "My heart was pounding like crazy," he said. "I thought they were going to say that he died, and I felt guilty almost because Heidi was supposed to have run too, and if he had been there we'd have pushed each other. Without Heidi, the victory seemed so empty."

The third day.

Cathy Guemple, a nurse, was working the 3:00-to-11:30 P.M. shift. While she was checking Heidi he opened his eyes for about two minutes. She hurried out of the intensive care unit and to the waiting area to fetch Merle and DeLoris. However, when they got to the room his eyelids were closed. He was asleep again. Nonetheless, it was a reason for optimism. The corner had been turned.

"We knew from then on it was going to be all right," Linda Heidenreich said after talking with her mother by phone. "Even though he was still on the critical list we gave thanks for the saving of Steve's life that night at a communion service. We started a prayer chain and we prayed for a complete healing, physical and emotional and spiritual.

"I can't remember the words we used to describe it but we asked big—real big. We dared to ask for a miracle."

The fifth day.

Sunday, March 21. Heidi developed pneumonia. But because of his strong lungs, Doctor Rak was able to treat it with antibiotics only.

The sixth day.

Monday, March 22. Almost imperceptibly, and for reasons not yet entirely clear, Heidi began to improve. He was removed from the critical list and his condition was changed to serious. A nurse sat him up in bed and he opened his eyes for approximately thirty seconds and turned his head when his name was called.

Later in the afternoon he responded to pain by making sounds, but he did not open his eyes. Roger visited in the evening and spoke to Steve, who opened his eyes and said, "Rog . . . !" The nurse in the room quickly answered, saying, "Hi, Steve!" Heidi replied, "What was that?" and then he closed his eyes and fell back. Roger excitedly rushed to the lobby to give the news to his parents and the entire waiting room erupted with joy. It was the most promising sign yet.

The eighth day.

Wednesday, March 24. Charges of driving while drunk and leaving the scene of an accident, both misdemeanor offenses, were filed in Monroe County Court in Bloomington against Sonny Thorsrud.

The ninth day.

Thursday, March 25. Ritalin was given orally to Heidi to help increase his periods of alertness. His chart:

> —4:00 P.M. Color good, skin dry and warm. Opens eyes upon command. Pupils equal in reaction to light. Does not grip hands. When asked if he had head pain, nodded and said, "Yes . . . help me."

Beth was scheduled to make the 6:00 P.M. visit. Returning from an early, leisurely dinner with her mother and the Heidenreichs, she walked into Steve's room to find Dr. Rak at the foot of the bed with a look of victory on his face. Heidi's eyes were open and he was staring at the ceiling and turning himself from side to side. He was out of the coma. The doctor sent word to the lobby to notify Merle and DeLoris, who immediately jumped up and rushed to the elevator. The three visitors all spoke at once, wanting to explain to Steve exactly what had happened to him. But he was not coherent, his eyes were glazed; the doctor pointed out to them that Heidi wasn't paying much attention.

As the three of them left the room, Merle felt strangely subdued. He was aware that Steve had been stimulated artificially with Ritalin and he would not allow himself to be artificially enthused. "There was no need for me to be depressed because things were coming along and the doctor hadn't said anything discouraging, but I don't know, I was just depressed," Merle remembers. "I'd go up there and there just wasn't any progress. I'd come down and everyone would want to know if he had said anything. I'd say no. And it had been that way for a while."

At 7:00 P.M., an orderly carried Heidi to a chair because he could not move his legs by himself. This was the same Heidi, world-class athlete, who precisely sixty days before had run a four-minute mile. He tried to push himself up from the chair and could not. His nurse looked at him sadly, shaking her head. She thought about his running and wondered if he would ever be able to run again.

Beth had been given permission for a 1:00 A.M. visit. When she left with Roger her stolid exterior cracked and the tears flowed. Roger wrapped his arms around her, holding her tightly for a few moments. He offered to buy her a drink. Beth nodded, and as they walked to a nearby bar, she told him a secret: She and Steve had planned to be engaged.

The tenth day.

Friday, March 26. Dr. Rak wrote in his progress report: "Stephen has made significant progress. He is more alert and he is saying more words."

Roger was still terribly worried, however. "I was sure at that point that he would live, that he would make it, but in what sense I did not know," he says. "We were told he would have problems with his memory and I assumed he would hardly be able to talk ever again. I saw him as an invalid . . . living in a nursing home or an institution."

He had visited Heidi and watched as his brother, unable to straighten his legs, again was helped to a chair. His eyes were closed and his head was flopped over on one shoulder. He began slipping, slowly, out of the chair and a nurse had to hurry to his side and lift him into bed. "It looked so hopeless I had to go," Roger recalls. Demoralized and disheartened, his emotional capacity exhausted, he flew back to Evanston.

The thirteenth day.

Monday, March 29. At 1:00 A.M. Heidi had been fed half a dish of vanilla pudding which he consumed with difficulty. He made no attempt to talk. During the next check, though, there was a change. The chart:

—3:00 A.M. Was definitely more alert. Shook head yes and no and said "uh huh" to a question. When asked if it hurt too much to talk, said, "Hurts too lot."

—8:30 A.M. Told briefly and simply of jaw surgery this afternoon. Seemed to understand. Responded positively when asked if he'd like to use a notebook and a pencil. Formed a few letters but unable to communicate anything meaningful and soon became frustrated and gave up.

—Noon. Coach Bell here. Does not recognize him. Sat up in chair with reluctance. Would prefer to sleep. Told again of surgery.

That afternoon, the bones of his lower jaw were set and wired shut.

Dr. Rak measured Heidi's progress without the benefit of Ritalin with one word: Remarkable. The doctor wrote, with much satisfaction:

He tries to write and he looks at magazines. His speech is sparse, probably due to his non-fluent aphasia [a refusal to make an attempt to speak].

Beth had brought a newspaper to Heidi. His eyes scanned the pages but he was holding the paper upside down and did not realize it because of spatial disorientation, a parietal lobe impairment.

Bell had located a portable television and, after permission was obtained to bring it into the intensive care unit for Steve, it was turned to the NCAA basketball championship game being played in Philadelphia. He saw the Hoosiers win, 86–68, being encouraged to take deep breaths by the nurses while he watched. Carol Schmidt, supervisor of the nursing staff in the unit, did her best to transform the event into a mini-party. Cheering, she urged, "Go Big Red!" and Heidi, his jaws wired now, feebly attempted to smile.

Later, Heidenreich remembered nothing of the evening. He was sleeping when the celebration began a few blocks from the hospital in the middle of the IU campus. There was bedlam; pandemonium. Some four thousand deliriously happy students crowded into the streets, many standing on tops of cars. Four freshly tanned young men, just back from Florida, stripped to the buff and danced for joy.

The fourteenth day.

Tuesday, March 30. Steve's progress had been stunning in the last two days, astounding even Dr. Rak, who decided to transfer his patient from the intensive care unit to the orthopedic and neurology wing the next day. Heidi had received a batch of mail and he wanted to walk for the first time. Two nurses assisted him to the bathroom. He walked to a scale and weighed himself, at first sitting on the scale. He would not let anyone else see what his weight was.

The fact that Heidenreich was a distance runner proved to be both an advantage and a disadvantage. An advantage when he developed pneumonia because his cardiovascular and pulmonary systems were in such superb shape and used to stresses that the new stress was not catastrophic. A disadvantage because he had little fat on his body. He was catabolic; he wasn't eating much and so he was using up his spare fat reserves. His frame, once muscle-defined, quickly took on the appearance of emaciation. His weight had dropped from 130 pounds to 115 in six days.

DeLoris Heidenreich had shown the nurses pictures of her son with a beard, a son with robust, hard-muscled, attractive features. What they saw now reminded them of a pitiable ninety-year-old, an invalid who, stooping, shuffled from his bed to the bathroom hanging on the arms of two nurses. With his shaved head he was described by one nurse as "looking like a refugee from Buchenwald."

That evening he sat up in a chair for fifteen minutes and nodded when asked if he wanted some Coke to drink. When the nurse handed him the cup he held it in his hands a few minutes, then threw it in the wastebasket without drinking any. He went back to bed and refused to walk any more, seeming upset and withdrawn. When asked if he wanted to move to the other floor, however, he nodded again.

Heidi was in his bed staring idly at the wall when Mark Schlundt suddenly appeared, having sneaked past the nurses and into the room. "Hi, Steve. How ya doin'?" asked Schlundt. Heidi rolled his head over and stared dumbly at Schlundt, who left, disappointed, when he could not make contact. He was astonished to see such a shrunken frame and thought to himself that Heidi resembled a baby bird in a nest.

As fragile as he might have seemed, Heidenreich was getting well. He was not accepting death, which might, in fact, have been his destiny. Those who knew him well, who knew a special spirit existed within this runner, knew that the fires still were burning deep within; that his rage to live was as real as his rage to run had been. Tomorrow he was to take one more step in the steps that would turn into miles. He was to leave the intensive care unit.

The miracle of Kinser Pike was about to begin.

9

Fourth Floor. Bloomington Hospital. April's promise had beaten the chill of March. The wait began anew for DeLoris Heidenreich and Beth Burnside. Merle had returned to Watertown to resume his teaching duties. He could not take more time to watch his son's progress although he wanted to. Now that Steve was out of intensive care, he felt, he could leave him to the expert ministrations of the hospital staff, and of his wife and family.

As for Steve, he did not react well to being transferred. He sat like a statue in a chair, staring fixedly and impassively ahead of him and refusing to acknowledge anyone. Heidenreich's doleful, infantile behavior was not entirely unexpected at this stage of his recovery. In many ways his emotional age approximated that of a toddler, a twenty-three-year-old toddler. He had just been plucked from his protective environment. He had left the security of surroundings and voices he had come to recognize and this new world was strange and unacceptable. Initially, at least.

There were new freedoms for him, however. He was beginning to feed himself. He could have visitors on a limited basis. And he was starting to string sentences together, even though some were elementary and confusing to the listener. This was because of another impairment—fluent aphasia, the loss of his ability to speak coherently.

He was in a world of his own. It was a world of pain, of frustration, of simplicity. He knew he was a runner. He knew he was a college student. He had been told many times that he had been hit by a car. Upon hearing this he nodded but he did not comprehend. This bright human being with high intellectual capacities had—in a matter of a few frozen moments of the screeching of tires and the sickening welding of body to metal—been reduced to a vulnerable childlike creature.

The mountain that rose in front of him now was not one that could be conquered with a stopwatch. It was an obstacle of much larger proportions. It meant a rebirth, a re-emergence.

His brain was scrambled; his syntax was screwy; his thought processes were anachronistic. His disorientation, the strange things he said, and his appearance, that of a ghostly, thin being who looked forty years older than his chronological age, startled his visitors, his friends, his teammates. And the dream of competing at Montreal had been shattered.

Heidi was deluged with mail from across the country, some of it from persons who had never met him or had never heard of him until the accident. A sampling of the letters he received at the hospital:
From Bloomington, Indiana.

Dear Steve:
Who has touched the sky
Who has seen the clouds as they went singing by
None but the few, the few who knew
The sun by its first name
The color of the moon.
There have been some who walked among us
Some who wore love like a child's smile
They touched the sky, met it eye to eye
Just like loving one another
For a little while.

Who has touched the sky?
Keep reaching high, Heidi
An IU student

From Bloomington, Indiana.

Dear Steve:
You're going to make it Steve, as my God is a faithful God who honors prayer. I expect that your life will be dramatically changed now and it can only get better. You see, you have great gifts of courage and boldness. I realize it must be hard to see this tragedy as anything good but perhaps some day you will look back and view the hours and days following the accident as your finest time. Why? Because you will have a new appreciation of yourself, of others, of life itself. Heidi, I've known you for years. I don't know where your track will go. I do know this. I care very much about Steve Heidenreich the person, the fun-loving, lighthearted Heidi. I always will. Get well!!!

Tuck

From Ralston, Nebraska.

Dear Steve:
Being a football player I have suffered many physical hurdles. Through it all I have kept a letter of courage at my side. You may have read this open letter from Cliff Cushman to the youth of his hometown, Grand Forks, North Dakota, before but I would like to share it with you.

CLIFF CUSHMAN'S LETTER
Don't feel sorry for me. You may have seen the U.S. Olympic Trials on TV September 13, 1964. If so, you watched me hit the fifth hurdle, fall and lie on the track in an inglorious heap of skinned elbows, bruised hips, torn knees and injured pride, unsuccessful in my attempt to make the Olympic team for the second time. In a split second all of the many years of training, pain, sweat, blisters and agony and running were simply and irrevocably wiped out. But I tried. I would rather fall flat knowing I had put forth an honest effort than never to have tried at all.

Over 15 years ago I saw a star—first place in the Olympic Games. I literally started to run after it. In 1960 I came within three yards of grabbing it; this time I stumbled, fell and watched it recede four more years away. There is nothing I can do about it now but get up, pick the cinders from my wounds and take one more step followed by one more and one more until the steps turn into miles and the miles into success.

I may never make it. The odds are against me but I have something in my favor—desire and faith. Romans 5:3–5 says, ". . . We rejoice in our sufferings, knowing that suffering produces endurance and endurance produces character and character produces hope and hope does not disappoint us . . ." At least I am going to try.

(Cliff Cushman, a University of Kansas athlete, was the silver medalist in the 400-meter intermediate hurdles at Rome in 1960. He is today on the list of those missing in action in Viet Nam.) From Bloomington, Indiana.

Dear Mr. and Mrs. Heidenreich:
We know there is little we or anyone can say to ease the grief caused by the tragedy that has happened to Steve. But we must express our extreme sorrow and heartfelt sympathy to both of you and we want you to know that the continuous prayers of our family and of our friends are for Steve, you and your family.
Sincerely,
Walter Thorsrud

While some of Heidi's visitors were alarmed and others felt pity upon seeing him for the first time, his family and Beth were enormously relieved that he had made it this far. Dr. Rak was elated. It was as if one hurdle had been vaulted and now there was a fresh set of realities to be conquered. Questions remained: Would his recovery be flawed? Would there be permanent brain damage and, if so, how much? Would he ever be "normal"—physically and mentally? In the sudden change in his fortune in the previous days the fight had turned and he seemed, to everybody, to carry the promise of life.

Through it all, the hospital staff was fascinated by the bravery of DeLoris Heidenreich. She was what held the family together. Yet in her private moments she knew that things were not ever going to be the same again. Her son had almost died. The thoughts of what life might have been like without him refused to go away. Although Steve had survived, the nightmares and the dread that haunted her were never going to disappear.

On April 1, the sixteenth day, Dr. Rak was a happy man. "Stephen has made unbelievable progress," he said at the time. "Head injury patients seem to go along not going anywhere and you get discouraged and then suddenly they do a lot better. He showed some facial expression when I talked with him and that was encouraging. It meant he was much better. He said he was unable to understand what he was reading and that was important because he was aware of his deficits. If he was aware of what he could not do it meant that he could then correct the inability."

Brain surgery and its aftermath are precarious. "He was getting better and it makes you feel good when you gamble and try to save somebody's life and then they respond," comments Dr. Rak, grinning happily. "Among the worst things that can happen to neurosurgeons is when they try and save a person's life and end up with a vegetative patient. You have put a lot of effort in and you've accomplished not a thing because it is very hard on the family. It strains their resources financially, emotionally and physically. It isn't hard on the patient because he's not aware of what is going on."

Each day the search was for something new that was good. There were still tears but emotions were calmer now. The family and friends kept each other going. Anything that was positive— anything—passed the spark, and everybody else caught it.

And that spark traveled around the nation. On March 17, the day that the news had filtered out of Bloomington on network radio reports and the wire services, Associated Press and United Press International, the reaction among runners was universal: Outrage. Grab the shotgun. The thing that all runners feared had occurred. Frank Shorter summed it up in a letter to Bell. "I've had dreams about this happening to me," he wrote. "Why is it that drivers become idiots when runners are on the roads?"

Steve Heidenreich was completely detached from this swirl of controversy. He was hungry, that was all he knew. Why could he not have steak? His mother sighed and pointed to his mouth; it was wired closed. Soup was not what he wanted day after day, but soup was what he got.

In the late afternoon and evenings his teammates visited. One of them, for old times' sake, thought to bring Heidi a Penguin malt.

Strawberry.

A Penguin became the price of admission for anyone who wanted to see him. At last, something he actually wanted to ingest that he could manage. "Malts!" Heidi cried. "More malts! We need more malts! Get some food in here . . ."

Heidi sipped all the Penguin flavors brought to him except peanut butter, since the nut chips tangled with the rubber bands in his mouth. Dean Reinke brought a chocolate malt. Like the teammates who found the sight of Heidi too painful to bear, Reinke did not stay long either. "It was very uncomfortable being in the room because you didn't know what the hell to say and you didn't know if he was understanding anything you said," recalls Reinke, who noticed on one visit that Heidi's arms were so thin that when he lifted one arm the watch he was wearing slid all the way to his elbow.

Sam Bell found the visits both amusing and distressing. Heidi's nonsensical, disjointed, frivolous statements evoked laughter and yet they illustrated poignantly to Bell how damaged his runner was.

Confused, Heidi said to Bell:

"Coach, I need a workout. Give me a workout.

"Coach, I'm gonna be so tough! I'm going to blow the drawers off that Craig Virgin. Coach, did you know I ran into a car; wasn't that stupid?"

DeLoris showed her son how to call for a nurse. Her efforts were wasted, though. Heidi would push all the buttons and lights would flash on everywhere. He would coax visitors to take him to the bathroom and insisted they help him find his pants. He told them he wanted to leave, to go to Nick's. His sneak missions to the bathroom put all personnel on military alert in the aftermath of one trek. Once behind the door, there was a loud THUD! His rubbery legs had given way.

On the sixteenth day, April 1, Heidenreich began physical therapy. His improvement, as recorded, was substantial.

April 1—Arrived in therapy department by wheelchair. He is able to transfer, stand, pivot, sit with minimal assistance. He walks with small steps and with a narrow-based gait.

April 3—Simon-sez activities. A high knee walk was initiated to help his balance.

April 5—Patient's strength and endurance continue to improve daily. He periodically has trouble following right-left directions. He was able to walk a distance of 75 feet and stand with assistance. He also was able to ascend and descend one flight of stairs but complained of pain in his legs when performing the activity.

April 8—Improved tremendously in endurance and strength. Now able to walk for increasingly longer distances. Working with weights for his upper and lower extremities.

Heidi ridiculed the light weights used in therapy. Mildly annoyed and blinded by his limitations he said, "Enough of this! Let's get down to some *real* lifting."

His impatience intrigued Nancy Weinberg, one of his nurses. "He was the first patient I had seen with a head injury who got better fast," she recalls. "Each day you could see the progress. It got to be fun to come in every day and see what had changed. One thing about him stayed the same. He was always hungry. We could not keep him filled up. Everybody who came to see him brought him a malt and it still wasn't enough."

Roger Heidenreich reluctantly agreed to return to be with DeLoris at the hospital. His father convinced him that he simply had to spend a weekend in Bloomington. When he got back to the hospital, his mother took him to Steve's room but did not tell him what to expect. Therefore, Roger was not at all ready for any startling revelation, or any marked difference from the last time he had seen him. While DeLoris waited in the hall he walked gingerly into the room.

There was his brother, who was sitting in a chair wearing a bathrobe and his Nike waffle trainer shoes. Heidi got up, slowly, and reached out a hand.

"Hi, Rog . . ."

It was an extraordinary moment, one that Roger would remember forever. He was exultant. His face glowed. Then he laughed, caught up in the passionate excitement of seeing his brother very much alive. Roger turned to his mother, who was standing in the hallway, beaming and also caught up in Roger's illumination.

"God!" he said to her, excitedly. "It's . . . it's incredible!"

Remembering more of that delicious moment later, Roger recalled: "He was wearing those silly wire frame glasses with this butch haircut and he was talking and you couldn't shut him up and nobody wanted to. It just blew my mind—I felt so good. I don't know if I put it in terms of religion but I thought it really was a miracle. Boy, did I feel good!"

And Heidi did, as well.

"Where's Schlundt?" he crowed. "Get me on a workout program . . . !"

Heidi demanded that his brother go with him to the bathroom. When they got inside, he said: "When do I get to go home? I'm going nuts. Good God, get my pants. Get me outta here . . . !"

The next day, Heidi was visited by his legal counsel, Tom Berry, who had only met Steve once before the accident. "This wasn't the same guy I had talked to at all; he was in a completely different world," Berry said afterward. "He had no idea who I was, that was clear, but he wanted to pretend he did. People told him he should. 'Your attorney is coming'—you know. He did not know what had happened to him. His conversation made absolutely no sense. He indicated several times that he was going to run that afternoon. He explained to me that he had been hit by a car as if it was some sort of joke that someone had played on him. My impression at that time was that he would not be a vegetable as I had been warned, but I did not think he would ever again attain enough mental stability to become a member of society because he was living in a fantasy world, a world of unreality, a world in which he was going to run tomorrow. The doctors assured me he could not compete again. He had surprised them by living and by being able to communicate, which he could do in a halting way. But he had no memory—none. He knew he was a runner and he was going to run tomorrow. Everything he said was so unreal that it was sad."

Afterward, Heidi remembered neither the weekend when his brother had visited him nor the meeting with Berry.

As soon as Dr. Rak was assured that there were not going to be surgical complications he decided to send Heidi home to Watertown to get him away from other sick patients—to get him into a familiar environment and routine where he could begin to try and organize thoughts.

The doctor felt Steve was ready, and this was due in great part to his running. People who run regularly develop hundreds of new capillaries that distribute oxygen to tissue and nerve cells and carry away metabolic waste products. Does a runner own recuperative powers with his additional blood vessels not possessed by non-runners? Did this explain Heidenreich's unexpected improvement? Why is it that some patients with head injuries progress and others languish in institutions and never do?

"Distance runners are like coiled springs," Dr. Rak explains. "They are ready to explode, move, do things, and I don't know whether this is a result of their running or whether their running is a result of the fact that they have to expend this inner energy. They are compulsive. They seem to have a drive that ordinary people do not. Often, patients recovering from head injuries lose their drive. They do not attempt to better themselves. They are quite content to sit and do nothing. Damage to the temporal lobe —a lesion like Heidi had—can destroy initiative. A person might be capable of achieving but he does not. He sits. Damage to the temporal or parietal lobes can also lead to impairment in recognition of patterns and can hamper a person's ability to reason.

"Stephen apparently has an intrinsic drive that was so strong that it maintained itself. Not all athletes have one this powerful. I mean, he really tried. He was one of the hardest-working people I have ever met, not only during his hospital stay but after he went home. Most people with head injuries sit in front of the TV and sip their soda pop and that is it. Stephen refused to accept this."

The news that Steve Heidenreich was to leave the hospital produced a variety of reactions—but in one way or another, everyone who heard about it was exhilarated.

The twenty-third day.

Thursday, April 8. Heidi was flown to Watertown in a private plane. His departure was a cause for celebration at Bloomington Hospital. He was a trailblazer, the first successful head-injury patient at the hospital. Administrator Roland (Bud) Kohr said of his progress, "It was like your ball team had won." Nurse Jo Anne Matavuli asked Heidi for his autograph. He signed "The Star" and told her that he was going home to prepare a steak and pizza. In the blender, naturally.

Sam Bell spared Heidi the glare of publicity by trying to insulate him. Nonetheless, a picture of him was taken at the airport as he boarded the plane at 12:30 P.M. and was printed on Friday in the *Indiana Daily Student,* the university newspaper. The camera had captured clearly the gaunt Heidi and his shaved head with bristly hair just starting to grow in. When the picture was sent to him later by Beth, he hid it and did not allow his parents to look at it.

Heidenreich had beaten odds that were said to be far too great to overcome. It was thought he would be hospitalized for many weeks. He was leaving on the twenty-third day. He had begun the comeback but he was by no means normal. He was walking but not well; his thinking was aberrant; his memory and his intellectual functions were impaired. He was not yet a human being. But as one of his nurses said, "It was the ending to a dream. We did it together, all of us, everyone, and it's going to take a lot of work on his part but maybe he can run again."

The lights were on far into the night at Tom Berry's office. On his desk were piled folders, tape recordings, police statements, briefs and dozens of pieces of notebook paper with jottings and memoranda filling the lines and margins.

He prowled about the room, moving from one window to the next. He was restless and eager to start the real work of this case. He was girding for battle. Stocky, short and with a modish air, he barked out his requests in short and concise sentences. He was a compulsive man and he had a tendency to punctuate his conversations with sweeping gestures, dropping his right hand with a chopping motion to emphasize a point. He worked hard and he enjoyed the material fruits of his labor.

A graduate of both Ohio State University and of the Indiana University School of Law, he was, by an auspicious bit of political freakishness, elected prosecuting attorney of Monroe County. When the lawyer who held that job moved to Florida, Berry was nominated as the Republican candidate to replace him. Berry was twenty-six years old and looked much younger. He was unknown and he was elected with fewer votes than any other Republican ever in Monroe County, but, at that, he buried his Democratic opponent. Four years later Berry was reelected in a landslide. When he left and returned to private practice he had compiled one of the highest conviction rates in the state of Indiana.

Berry walked to his desk, let himself down into a large leather chair and took in one hand the microphone from a dictation machine. He began, "Memo . . . Heidenreich file. The question before us is whether runners constitute an undue menace on a public street. If they do, then by God the drunk driver sure as hell does!"

Berry had filed a $500,000 damage suit against Sonny Thorsrud for Heidenreich. He correctly surmised that his case was fraught with juridical hazards. Convincing a jury could be difficult because of a contributory negligence clause in Indiana law that disallows a complainant to collect damages if he contributes what a judge or jury believes to be a minimum of one per cent to the accident.

Berry knew that Heidenreich had for the past nine years not missed more than ten days of running and that in those thousands of miles he always had run facing traffic. That was the side of the street where his body was found on March 16.

Still, Berry expected the defense in the Heidenreich case to remind a jury repeatedly that Heidenreich might have been running in the middle of the road. Heidenreich himself had no memory of where he had been. Additionally, Berry knew that a jury might include one or two persons who are irritated by runners on the streets.

Berry poked through the pile of material on his desk. Sorting out the details of the events on the night of the accident in his mind, he was certain that he could tie Sonny Thorsrud to it. If only he could identify two persons seen bending over Heidi's body on Kinser Pike. He had reason to believe they held all the answers.

Three IU students returning home after a movie that night at about 11:45 happened to turn south on Kinser Pike. As they reached the top of an incline, some 150 feet from where Heidi was hit, they saw two young men get out of a car and walk toward an object in the street. One of the students, John Dierks, who was driving, told police he thought the car was a yellow Dodge Dart. As Dierks slowed, he and his friends were shocked to see a body lying in the street.

"Christ!" exclaimed Dierks. "I don't believe it. Look at the blood! It's on the curb, on the street. Look at the guy's face! There's blood all over!"

Paul Rau, sitting in the back seat, nodded and whistled softly. "Man," he said, "that's awful. Are those two going to help him? I guess they are."

Dierks drove off. He told police later that the car, parked facing south about three feet in front of Heidi's body, had Indiana license plates. Two of the three students remembered that the car's lights were off. Dierks thought he remembered that one of the young men was wearing a baseball cap.

The 10:00 P.M.–6:00 A.M. shift is, for the most part, routine for Bloomington police officers. The Heidenreich hit-and-run was not routine, though. Before the night was over it had involved nearly every officer and detective on duty, and the investigation mushroomed into one of the most exhaustive that veteran Bloomington policemen could recall. People in the community took sides and the issue of who was at fault became an uncomfortable, highly emotional one.

The 1970 beige-colored Plymouth Duster that Sonny Thorsrud drove to the Bloomington Police Department in the early morning hours of March 17 was examined by officers Becky Holder and Todd McCormick, and by John Gaston, who went to the station as soon as he had finished his shift at the emergency room of the hospital. He brought Heidi's running clothes and shoes with him to the station.

There were two dents in the hood of Thorsrud's car. One was eight inches long and deep, near the front. The other, not as large, was closer to the windshield. Gaston noted that both appeared to be cleaner than the surrounding areas on the hood, which indicated that they had been made recently.

Paint samples from the car, rusted metal pieces with a layer of beige paint found on the west side of Kinser Pike and to the south of Heidi's body, a mud sample, pieces of rubber collected at the accident scene, a blue plastic strand, and a single animal hair on one of the fenders were tagged and later sent for analysis to the FBI lab in Washington.

Curiously, Thorsrud was permitted to drive his car back home, and the police did not impound it until 11:25 A.M. on March 17, eight hours later. The car was then driven by police to a city-owned garage and roped off. A cardboard sign placed on the hood warned: "DO NOT TOUCH."

The plastic strand, similar to that on a large roller in an automatic car wash, triggered a mild debate among the officers. "When I looked at the car sitting in front of the station I swore it had been washed," said Todd McCormick. "It was cleaner than a whistle." John Gaston disagreed and Detective Patty Burns sided with Gaston.

From their interviews, police were able to fit together a sequence of Sonny Thorsrud's movements on March 16. Thorsrud had met Marvin Thornton at Games Ltd., a pinball emporium, between 7:30 and 8:00 P.M. and they had driven in Thornton's car to the Tau Kappa Epsilon fraternity where they visited a friend, Jim Wilmes. "We sat in my room and watched TV for two hours and drank," Wilmes told police lieutenant Frank Allen.

"Drank what?" Allen wanted to know.

"Jack Daniel's whiskey and Seven-Up. In root beer mugs."

"Did Thorsrud drink more than the rest of you?"

"I'd say he did. He had three or four full glasses."

The three emptied a bottle of Seven-Up quickly and drove to

a grocery store for more. When they returned they sat in the car and smoked a joint of marijuana. The fraternity had scheduled an exchange dance with a sorority that evening and they decided to go.

"Was there beer available?" Allen asked Wilmes.

"Yes. In kegs."

"And then what happened?"

"We drank some beer and danced. After a while they left."

"What kind of shape was Thorsrud in?"

"Marvin seemed okay and I thought Sonny was the same until I heard later that something happened. Sonny must have been sort of drunk."

"Can you describe for me what Thorsrud was wearing?"

"Sonny had his hat. He left it in my room. He's usually wearing one when I see him. He's got a lot of hats. We used it to put ice in."

"What kind of hat is it?"

"Baseball."

Thorsrud and Thornton returned to Games Ltd. minutes after it had closed at eleven o'clock. Thornton knocked on the window and one of the employees let him in. Thorsrud was sitting in the back seat of Thornton's car. Another employee, George Wilson, left to get a pizza and as he did he saw Thorsrud attempting to get out of Thornton's car. He was wobbling. When questioned, Wilson guessed it was 11:40 when he himself left.

"When you got back to Games Ltd. were Thornton and Thorsrud there?" asked Allen.

"No. Both cars were gone."

The time that Thornton gave police that he left for home did not coincide with Wilson's story. Thornton said he departed alone at 11:30, before Thorsrud.

"What do you think about Thorsrud's condition to drive a car?"

"Bad," said Thornton.

"What makes you feel that way?" asked Allen.

"I don't know. He was just drunk."

Carefully, Tom Berry sifted the information that had been gathered and began formulating his own hypotheses. There were no paint flecks or smears on Heidi's clothing that could conclusively pin the Thorsrud car to the accident. A palm print lifted from the hood did not match Heidenreich's. Skid tests made with Thorsrud's car did not match tire tracks on Kinser Pike.

A rumor flashed through Bloomington on Wednesday the 17th that Heidi was stooping and tying his shoe laces when he was struck a glancing blow by one car and then was hit by a second car as he lay unconscious. Unlikely, decided Berry. There were no tire impressions, no grease or oil, or any debris from the underside of a car on his sweat clothes.

Had Heidi been tying his shoes he most likely would have been struck full force by the bumper or grill. But the only markings on his back were a deep contusion and abrasions on the left side. His knees were scraped but this might have been the result of his fall to the road.

Berry studied Becky Holder's report. In it she had mentioned that William Thorsrud said his son had awakened him at 1:00 A.M., then amended his story to make the time midnight. What happened to that hour? Berry wondered. Did Sonny Thorsrud drive around aimlessly for an hour before going home? And who was the second person bending over Heidi's body?

Heidenreich's skull was split open on the right side. His sweat bottoms were scuffed on the left side and the deep contusion, a possible point of impact, was on the left side of his back. Was he returning on Kinser Pike to the apartment from his run rather than just leaving? Berry thought not. If he were struck by a southbound auto he would have been running on the right side of Kinser Pike, with traffic, which was not his habit.

Berry strongly suspected that Heidi was in flight with both feet off the ground when he was hit. His body was flipped onto the hood by the impact. His body then probably slid off the car and crashed to the street, his head cracking against the curb.

Berry brooded about the conflicting details, and then summoned Sonny Thorsrud and his father to appear for depositions. He was eager to see what they would say. Sworn testimony under penalty of perjury could perhaps clear up the murky waters. Berry brought a thick file with him.

"What time did your son get home?" he asked William Thorsrud.

"The best I can remember it was between 11:30 and 11:45."

"How do you know that?"

"I heard him come in and I glanced at the clock. It was a week night and we don't like him to stay out late."

William went on to explain that he had called out to him and asked him what it was that he wanted. His wife, who also was awakened, got up with her husband.

"He acted kind of frightened," said William. "He said he had heard something hit his car on the way home and he'd looked at it when he got home and there was a dent in it and he didn't know whether something hit him, a dog or what. He was quite a bit upset. We talked about it. I went out and looked at the car and there were a couple of places where he hit or something had hit him. We were trying to decide what to do. So we decided that we'd just get in my car and go back the route that he came home and when we got to where he heard the noise we'd see if there was something there."

What Thorsrud, his wife and son found on Kinser Pike were police barricades, police cars, red flashing lights, and spectators milling about.

"I stopped the car and walked up to a police officer and asked if there had been an accident and he said yes, that a jogger had been hit," said William Thorsrud.

Berry interrupted. "I imagine your heart stopped about this point, didn't it?"

"You bet it did."

The interrogation shifted to Sonny Thorsrud. He was a good athlete, heavily muscled and sturdy. He sat stone-faced awaiting Berry, who cleared his throat and began by asking his whereabouts on the night of March 16. Sonny said that he and Marvin Thornton had gone to Jim Wilmes's room at the TKE house.

"Jim said he had something for us to drink. I think it was Jack something, some sort of whiskey or something. He said we needed Seven-Up so we all went in Jim's car to get it.

"Then they went—they had a marijuana cigarette and they lit that. I was in the back seat and they passed it around once and I said I didn't want any more."

"Had you ever smoked marijuana before?"

"Yes."

Berry paused. "To your knowledge, are the things you said on tape at the police station on the night of the accident accurate? Did you tell the truth?"

"Most of it," said Thorsrud, looking away.

Berry paused again. "Tell us about the part that wasn't the truth."

"Well, they asked if I'd been drinking and I said no."

"How long did you stay at Games Ltd. before you took off in your car?"

Thorsrud answered haltingly. "Five to ten minutes."

"You really don't know, do you?" said Berry icily.

"From five to ten minutes. I think I was told that Steve was found a little before twelve, and I got home around 11:30 or 11:35."

"Which was it?"

Thorsrud said his memory was weak. "It was 11:30 or 11:35."

"When you left for home you turned north on Kinser Pike, as I understand it. You have testified that you heard a bump. Do you know where they found Steve?"

"Yes, I do."

Berry did not want to be accused of leading his witness. He phrased his next question slowly.

"Do the two coincide—the impact point and the place where Steve was found?"

"No."

"Where was the noise?"

"About thirty yards south of Steve."

"You talked to your father and what you said worried your folks enough to think that you might have hit somebody, isn't that true?"

"Right. We went out and looked at the car."

"You don't go back to the scene for a dog or a cat, right?"

"Right, well—yes."

"So your fear was that you had hit a person? That's true, is it not? Or it certainly was your parents' fear?"

"True."

To assist him in bolstering his case, Berry hired Arne Bergh, a forensic consultant in Bloomington who once was a crack private investigator of the Royal Canadian Mounted Police and director of the RCMP crime bureau. In the course of his investigative interviewing, Bergh found out that Sonny Thorsrud talked to Ann Cunningham, a former girlfriend, at school the morning following the accident. Marvin Thornton butted into their conversation and, as he did, Thorsrud walked away. Berry deduced that Thorsrud had not told him everything when he was questioned. Further, Berry still did not know whether Thorsrud was one of the two phantom youths, one wearing a baseball cap, reported by John Dierks to be bending over Heidenreich's body.

Bergh took more paint samples from Thorsrud's Plymouth Duster and a few weeks later phoned Berry with the news that the FBI was unable to match the rusted metal pieces with either paint or rust particles from the car.

Berry looked over Sonny Thorsrud's first sworn deposition for discrepancies and inconsistencies. The attorney summoned him again for testimony, and on the appointed day Thorsrud sat down in front of the lawyer and nodded respectfully.

"To this day do you know or do you have a theory about what you actually hit if it wasn't Steve?" began Berry.

"No, I don't," said Thorsrud.

"You did not stop your car . . . ?"

Thorsrud shook his head negatively. "I slowed it down. I never came to a complete stop."

Berry, attempting to establish a link to the baseball cap, asked Thorsrud about his clothing on the night of the accident.

Thorsrud frowned in recollection. "Well, I can guarantee you I had jeans on. That's about as much as I can remember."

"Did you have your baseball cap on?"

"I know I had one in the car. I don't know if I had one on at the time."

"You usually wear one, don't you?"

"Yes."

Berry then established the fact that Thorsrud had, some time after the Heidenreich incident in March, been charged with reckless driving. He had told police at that time that he had been drinking. Scarcely stopping for breath, Berry went into the Ann Cunningham matter.

"Did you talk with her after the accident?" said Berry, walking toward Thorsrud.

"Yeah. A little bit."

"She continued to be a close personal friend even after your romance sort of faded, didn't she?"

"For maybe a month or so."

Here, Berry gambled. He moved into the next question cautiously.

"It was rather an emotional scene, this talk you had with Ann Cunningham at the school, wasn't it?"

Thorsrud squirmed in his chair. "Yeah. I remember her crying."

"She tried to comfort you . . . tried to make you feel better."

"I suppose she did."

"What did she tell you?"

"That it would be all right."

"Your girlfriend was not crying because you hit a dog, was she?"

"She was crying because she knew I was upset."

"Why were you upset?"

"Because I thought I hit a person."

Berry stared at Sonny Thorsrud. The room was electric with tension.

"You told her that, didn't you?"

"Yeah. I thought I had hit Steve."

10

Afghan hounds. Sports cars. Yachts. Contact lenses. Peppermint soap. Incongruous as they were, these elements comprised a small child's world, the one Steve Heidenreich entered when he returned home from Bloomington Hospital. Watertown embraced him and shared in the joy of his family. A native son was home again, not as a conquering hero at the Olympic Games as many had envisioned him, but as a conqueror nonetheless. He brought with him not a medal but his life; he had laughed at the odds. To many, that in itself was a performance of Olympic proportion.

The private twin-engine plane circled the Watertown airport and started its descent in a long, smooth glide path. The pilot was careful not to drop too fast out of the sky and create a jarring change of pressure on one of his passengers. The pilot had received clearance to make the trip from Bloomington to Watertown at an altitude where the pressure would not be too great.

It was late afternoon and Broadway was moderately busy on this sun-splashed Thursday as the car, returning from the Watertown airport, came to a stop in front of the Heidenreich home. As Steve got out he said to his mother:

"I want to walk."

She looked at him. "Now . . . ?"

"I want to walk," he repeated emphatically.

DeLoris Heidenreich calculated that if her weariness in any way matched that of her son he could walk maybe twenty-five or thirty steps to the corner and back and that would be it.

"Okay," she agreed. "Let's walk."

She was wrong. When her son got to the corner he did not stop. His faltering steps, slow and somewhat halting, continued. He trudged around the entire block.

And so it began.

The days ahead were filled with similar walks—and with talks —as Steve groped to regain his mental balance in the healing process that his body was going through and as his mother, always, at his side guided him.

Which was as it had to be. Steve's behavior was that of a "happy two-year-old" when he first arrived home, his actions similar to those of a toddler. As Heidi progressed in the final eight months of 1976 and reached new stages, his "age" progressed also. But until late autumn he probably did not advance past age fifteen in his emotional stability. He remained immature and, at times, churlish. He pouted, he shouted, he blew his stack at the slightest provocation. He demonstrated, in other words, all the fragile personality signs that make up the "terrible teens."

There were reasons for this, of course. Pain tore at him when he had to yawn and he could not because his jaws were pulling at the wires. His frustration and bitterness were just beginning to grow. He complained of constantly feeling cold and he bundled up in a bulky sweater and a jacket. On his head was a blue stocking cap to hide his close-cropped, wiry butch. He wore the cap everywhere, to the laundromat and grocery store and library and even in the house.

He demanded his mother's attention constantly. When she washed the dishes he stood next to her. When she hung clothes in the back yard he stood nearby, exhibiting the possessiveness of a toddler.

He developed hyperacusis, a sensitivity to noise, probably because of an injury to a nerve in the middle ear. If the TV was on he switched it off, annoyed. If his sister Laurie, then thirteen, had her portable radio turned up to a level he thought irritating he often picked it up and threw it at her, a tantrum befitting a thirteen-year-old—which his mother thought his "age" to be a month or so after he came home. Near the end of April he was chagrined to discover pimples popping out on his face and back. He and his mother were confused by this but the acne also seemed to fit his "adolescence."

Heidi remembered little of his days in the hospital. One of his contact lenses had been knocked loose and lost in the accident and the Bloomington police had custody of his other lens. He brooded incessantly about the safety of the lens and of the peppermint soap in his apartment. He acquired, for some reason, an affinity for Afghan hounds.

Each morning, as soon as the breakfast dishes were put away, Steve called "Mom!" and DeLoris would know that it was time to go for a walk. Steve walked slowly but this did not bother her ("He always did walk slow; he is the only one in the family I can keep up with," she once said) because it meant she was always at his side, there to catch him if he stumbled. They returned for lunch and then, with typical impatience, he was ready to walk again in the afternoon. They strolled the sidewalks from one side of town to the other. DeLoris totaled the distances they walked for Dr. Rak, the longest being six miles. Their conversations meandered. They touched on track, the accident and Heidi's desire to begin lifting weights. He instructed her on how she should remodel the kitchen. He often asked for information on the accident.

"Tell me again, Mom, about the car."

"Steve, you were hit while you were running. That's why one of us has to be with you all the time, for your protection. Your head could easily be damaged if you were to fall down."

"Can I run?" asked Steve, who discounted pretty much what people told him of the accident. To this day he cannot recall any of the details.

"Not right away," replied his mother. "The doctor said you

could walk and you could lift some weights. He said you were to stay off motorcycles."

"Mom . . . can I have an Afghan hound?"

DeLoris Heidenreich sighed.

On the telephone, Heidi said little to either Dr. Rak or Sam Bell. He did not remember the doctor; he did Bell. "It was like talking to a five-year-old on the phone" says Dr. Rak. "There were long, silent gaps after I asked him a question. He seemed to be off in another world but I could hear him breathing so I knew he was still on the other end. Despite this I was amazed at the amount of walking he was doing. It was unexpected."

Bell was sobered by their talks. "It was hard for me to listen," he said. "His conversations were shallow and juvenile and that really bothered me. I was not sure how far back he would be able to come or how much of his equilibrium he would be able to regain."

Beth Burnside had started back to her classes in Bloomington. She began sending a barrage of letters to Steve that spurred him to write. He approached this exercise with doggedness but his letters were painful to read, shockingly elementary and vapid, and he could not remember what he had written from one letter to the next.

The first letter was a child's scrawl:

I'm glad you came to see me at the hospital. I only remember you a couple days I was so mixed up at the hospital. I'm glad

to be out of there. It is
nice good to be in
Watertown. I'm glad you are
doing well in school. It
is hard to believe your
going to graduate. That
must really be nice.
I'm getting to feel
better and can walk
really good

It must be nice to have a
nice car like you do. When
are you going to come see
me. I hope soon. I got
some new shoes some adidas
and some mike. I also saw
the papers that you sent

me. I sure hope you do well at SIU. I hope you come see me soon.

Love,

Steve

Some day I want to get an afghan hound.

Near the end of April, though, his letters began to show more depth. The spelling and punctuation continued to be poor but the scrawl was disappearing and the letters had more substance. He wrote:

Hi Beth,
I am starting to remember more. Do you remember the courses I took in spring semester. Do you know my teachers names. I remember I had some good teachers. I remember taking investment class and a class on the stock market and another business class I took from an old teacher who was really nice. I remember taking history in front of your house. I used to know a lot about the stock market.

I hope my ears and jaws get better. I hope my head gets better too. I haven't been sleeping well, to many stay up and to late and leave the lights on and watch tv. Sometimes I feel so tired I am afraid of falling down. I don't get much sleep. Two days ago I got a headache that lasted for three hours. Believe it or not I am getting pimples again. Not looking as good as I used to. Are you looking forward to seeing me. Even though I look terrible. My hair is so short and my jaws hurt so bad I can't talk much. That's why I can't call you. I hope you can take care of me when I go to Bloomington. Well Beth I am getting old and poor isn't that terrible. I sure wish I could afford a new stereo and an afgahn hound and a nice sports car. The hospital says I can only have more bills. I'm just kidding.

Love,
Steve

Beth answered by gently cautioning Steve on some of the problems he was experiencing. She encouraged him and she instructed him in a sort of surrogate-mother way, urging him to get more rest. And then she went on, hoping he would understand:

I was talking to a friend from Indianapolis about you tonight. She really feels that God has something special planned for you. Your recovery has been such a miracle. Life can so easily and quickly be taken away and yet yours was saved. Don't you think there's a reason for that? I do. I know that sounds silly coming from me, who you've always known as not a strong believer but in the last five weeks I've grown to believe in God again. I'm so grateful to Him for saving you.

Do you remember our second date, the day you came home from Russia? We went to Time Out and danced. While we were dancing we talked about how lucky you were to have gotten to go to Russia. All sorts of thoughts were going through my head but mainly I was thinking how special you were and wondering if God had a special plan for you. I said to you, "I wonder how you got so lucky?" and you looked at me and said, "I wonder . . ." Maybe it is only luck but even so—why are you so lucky? There's got to be a reason that things always go well for you. Try and think of the unique things you have to offer humanity and figure out what God's mission for you might be. I'm sure it will present itself in time.

Love,
Beth

At that moment Steve was not looking far ahead, not any more than a day or two at the most. Yet some weeks later he wrote Beth that he had a goal, "To help people. So many people have so many problems. I know I can't solve them all. I am only human but I can try to help some of them."

It was one evening in late April when Steve was in the bathroom that he was able, finally, to connect the many facts he had been told of his involvement in the accident with himself. Looking in the mirror he was distraught to find that the right side of his head was concave, as if someone had taken a hammer and bashed in the skull. He was terrified. He felt the indentation and shivered.

He went in to his mother and cautiously running a hand along the side of his skull he said, "I've got something to show you. There's something funny about me." For perhaps the hundredth time, DeLoris explained to him. For the first time he accepted it, believing finally that he had been in an accident and understanding that was why he was at home now. "Boy, I've got to be careful don't I?" he said, touching his head again.

"Yes," answered his mother. "You sure do."

Heidi's brain had shrunk. The swelling had decreased and as it did the scalp covering the section of skull that Dr. Rak removed pulled tight. It gave him a gruesome, eerie appearance.

"The sight can be upsetting to a patient," explains Dr. Rak. "They can see the injury area pulsating and they know that underneath that is the brain. It can be like a science fiction movie." DeLoris was thankful that Steve's apprehensions had been lessened. She took the opportunity to outline the details of more surgery in Bloomington in July, when a protective piece was to be inserted in his head. From that evening on there were no more doubts for Heidi. He accepted.

Now that he was home his neighbors and friends and even some of his former high school track opponents bombarded DeLoris and Merle with offers of assistance. The Heidenreich family had been hit with whopping medical costs. There seemed no more appropriate way to help a stricken runner than with a jogathon, an event in which a sum of money was pledged on a person for each lap that he ran.

In Sioux Falls, runners at Lincoln High School, which was Watertown's biggest rival in track and field when Heidenreich was a star, raised $696.25. In Watertown, a similar benefit was held at the city's stadium and was sponsored by the Watertown Quarterback Club.

The Watertown runners raised $3,075.78. Dwight Struckman, once Heidi's cross-country coach, ran thirty-three laps, as did Chuck Van Gerpen, a Watertown real estate agent whose pledges alone produced $711. The checks from both benefits were presented to Heidenreich later during a track meet. Heidi sat and watched some of the races but went home with his mother early, saying he was tired and cold.

As the Heidenreich car bumped across the railroad tracks on Fourth Street, the fusillade of sounds from the track meet alive in his ears, Steve suddenly turned to his mother with the matter now uppermost in his mind—Beth. She was coming to visit.

"Will she like me?" said Steve.

His mother laughed.

"Of course she will. Why would you say such a thing?"

"I don't talk very well. I can't get my mouth open. Beth might make fun of my head. I'm going to leave my hat on."

If Beth could have overheard this exchange she might have allayed Steve's fears and, at the same time, expressed to DeLoris a few of her own.

The Steve Heidenreich that she knew had vanished. She had not been able to talk with him in the hospital; none of what he said made sense. The closest part of her life was ended. However, as the jet settled to a soft touchdown at the Watertown airport, Beth had pretty much convinced herself that a new part of their relationship was about to begin—that during their separation Steve had, with the wave of a magic wand, become as before. The Steve she knew.

It was not so. His jaw was still large and he was, much to her disappointment, not appealing. He still seemed very childlike in many ways. But early in her ten-day stay her regret gave way to a comforting security. She felt—she was sure—that he would be a whole person again.

She was comfortable until one day when one of his tangled sentences came out discombobulated and Beth and Laura laughed uproariously. Furious, he clobbered Beth with a round-house right on the arm. It was then that Beth saw how much was trapped inside, how much frustration was festering and churning.

After Beth flew home, Heidi picked up his pen and wrote letters again. Practicing. Practicing. The words did not come easily. He sat and pondered, searching for the right one. But he thought his struggling was normal now.

Humiliated, he apologized to Beth for punching her, writing:

> I'm sorry I gave you a hard time when you were here. I realize I lose my temper fast and get upset easily. It is going to take a while for me to get over all of this. I have to take it easy and stay rested so I can recover.

Beyond their relationship and his letters, the next matter of business was his neglected schoolwork. He had lugged his books home with him and he confidently expected to make up the incomplete grades his professors had given him in the aftermath of the accident. He began sitting in the sun with a book under a willow tree in the backyard, sheathed in a sweater and a blanket. He flipped through the pages of his history and business tests. His eyes lingered on the printed words. He read them once . . . twice . . . but he did not comprehend. Shaking his head, he got up, climbed the back steps, opened the door and stuck his nose inside. Over the whir of the sewing machine he yelled at his mother: "I read it but it doesn't stick. If I read it again, it still doesn't make any sense."

Heidi put down his books and ignored them. There was no pressure on him and he figured that the real reason he could not fathom these printed illusions was because he was not sitting in a classroom. He was sure that once back at IU the words would make sense.

Curiously, Heidenreich had retained his arithmetical concepts. Numbers he could manage, words he could not, possibly because of his aphasia. Brain-damaged persons can sometimes manage to write though they cannot read, or can understand numbers and not letters. While he was in the hospital he had amazed his mother one morning by reciting the conspicuous portions of a lecture that he had attended on March 16, the day he was struck. This bit of recall was like a tiny island in the middle of the Pacific Ocean. The rest of his recent memory had been obliterated.

E. Roy John, writing in *Psychology Today* magazine, suggests: "Remembering requires the average pattern of a great many cells, not the dependable activation of any one cell. It is not the location of the cells that matters but rather the rhythm at which they fire. When we learn something, small groups of cells do not form new connections. Rather, cells in many parts of the brain learn a new rhythm of firing corresponding to the learning."

The functions in the damaged area of Steve's brain appear to have been picked up by other components of his brain. There appears to be no localization of activity. Cells work together. Patients with severe brain damage can recover lost functions completely. If there was localization this would not be possible because destroyed brain cells do not regenerate.

Given the source of Heidenreich's injury, a tear in the temporal lobe, his doctor was surprised that he was not displaying typical symptoms of destroyed initiative. He was, in fact, displaying tremendous initiative. He was fighting the odds.

The twin forces of pride and determination were at work here and they combined with the inexplicable compulsion a runner has to run. When a runner can see himself in his mind's eye loping easily in the twilight of a summer evening alone on a shaded forest path, his nostrils sensitized by the smell of pine needles, his solar plexus tightens in anticipation. This kind of attitude drove Heidi to pursue a part of himself that the accident had not removed. His obsession was born out of what had been denied him. He was restless. His longing to run ignited a blaze that was not extinguishable.

He went to the track. As his mother walked beside him he plodded resolutely on the same cinder oval where once strong legs had carried him so swiftly. At the top of one curve of the track stood Vic Michelson, his coach in high school, watching Steve walk slowly. His eyes misting, Michelson turned away. It was virtually impossible to accept that this fleshless young man was the same who on those spring days five years ago had made a mockery of the stopwatch, his strength of mind and legs destroying the workouts, ripping through them, while his teammates watched in wonder. Oh, how he remembered. Heidi running quarters. Heidi running.

Heidenreich began lifting weights at a health center in town owned by Don Robinson, who became a jogging partner at the municipal golf course. Heidi chose the course because it was peaceful. He told his mother he wanted to avoid the track at the stadium since he was fearful of a collision with the many young runners at practice.

In the next weeks Robinson ran often with Heidi, who shambled along at a ten-minute-mile pace, and in so doing was able to talk through his wired teeth.

In a wave of emotions, Heidi alternately showed his impish wit and spoke damningly of whomever it was that hit him. When he tired they stopped running. Rarely did they go more than two miles. If a wind blew up, Heidi did not run at all. He complained that he could feel it blow through his scalp, the only cover over the large chunk of skull that had been removed from the right side of his head.

On May 19 the dentist removed the wires from Heidenreich's mouth ("There were enough to cover up the hole in my head," said Heidi in jest) and that made his running easier. He could breathe freely through both his mouth and nose.

"C'mon, Ma," he said urgently one day at the golf course soon after the wires were off.

"Oh no you don't. Not me!"

"C'mon, Ma. We're going to run."

"You're crazy."

"No I'm not . . . no I'm not, Ma. I'll go slow. I promise. C'm-o-n-n-n-n."

DeLoris Heidenreich buckled under his relentless pressure. In her pants suit she gallantly, intrepidly, took a few mincing steps forward. One leg. Now the other.

She ran.

She walked.

She ran.

She walked. She stopped. Gladly.

"C'mon, Ma," coaxed her son, prancing in a circle around her. "Just c'mon . . ."

The novelty of this activity ebbed quickly, but she was excited by her son's enthusiasm.

Unencumbered at last by the wires on his jaws, Heidi happily looked forward to the thick, juicy morsels of meat that had been forbidden him. For an evening meal DeLoris grilled steaks, given to Steve as a gift, that had been sitting in the freezer. Heidi attacked them eagerly. But he put his fork down after one bite, a look of boyish hurt on his face. His tender jaw was so sore from disuse that he might as well have been chewing on a piece of leather. Until his jaw strengthened he existed on salads and soup and malts.

It was June. Before the month was out Heidi was to go back to Bloomington for surgery on his skull. As the days slipped away he attempted to answer the voluminous amounts of mail he had received from all parts of the nation. In Bloomington, Beth finished the work for her degree in business and got a job at a women's clothing shop as a stopgap measure. She had wanted a job in a bank that fit her career plans but there was none available. She quit looking and made the mistake of telling Steve so. In a reply he showed her no compassion. His own tough-mindedness showed through. The harshness evident in his letter was soon to dissipate, though.

Dear Beth,

Am I mad at you. You gave up so easy. The reason you won't get a good job in Bloomington is that you are not trying. Have you applied at every business in Bloomington that needs a business major? Have you applied at every bank in Bloomington? No you haven't. Are you persistent? Are you hustling? No you aren't because it is so hard to find a good job in Bloomington. If I quit as easy as you do I would not have finished any of my classes or run a step because it is so hard. Have you stopped smoking and been running or swimming? No you haven't. You are a loser because you always take the easy way out. Get your act together. I think I am a strong man. I need a strong woman. I hate to lecture to you but I think I need to paddle your butt. When we are married there is no way you can smoke or get out of shape like you have. So you better get it together. I wouldn't be lecturing if I didn't know you.

Love,
Steve

Heidenreich was as hard on himself as he was on Beth. He was supposed to wait until October to resume strenuous workouts, but he began them in August following his return to Bloomington. By then his zeal was at a fever pitch.

That there were other passions astir in his recuperation was plainly evident in a letter to Beth he wrote while he was in Watertown.

Am I getting horny. I hope you are. I will want to make love four times a day. I am serious. If you are as foxy as I am hoping, we will make love four times a day. So work hard at becoming foxy.

Impotency can be a serious consequence of brain damage. A human's sexuality is located in the brain's limbic system bordering, as it does, on the underlying brain. "We know that patients can have sexual difficulties following surgery but usually they are listed as psychological," explains Dr. Rak. Apparently, Steve wasn't troubled by a loss of libido.

Only once did Heidenreich mention to Beth his dashed Olympic hopes or the fear that he might never again be able to run at world-class level. He wrote: "I watched the NCAA track meet today. CBS said I was hit by a car. Now I'm known nationwide. I wish I was known as a champion. Anyway, I wish I could get back to Indiana. I want to see my friends."

On June 26, a Saturday, Heidi was on his way. Mark Schlundt met him at the Indianapolis airport and that night some forty of his friends welcomed him back to Bloomington. Uncharacteristi-

cally, though, after expressing to Beth the desire for the camara-
derie of his friends, he was cool. He told her later he wished that
there had been no party. He said he didn't feel up to one.

The following day, a Sunday, was not of historical significance
other than that it was the day of the 1,500-meter final at the
United States Olympic Trials in Eugene, Oregon. The first three
finishers assured themselves of a place on the American team
going to Montreal.

Four years, or more, is a long time to get ready for one day.
But this is the U.S. method of selecting its team. Surviving on this
cutthroat basis leaves little margin for error. World record-hold-
ers and runners leading the world in their events at the time of
the Trials have been left off the team because in the finals—on
that one day—they finished fourth. Luck is a factor. A runner can
train for four years and step off the curb and twist an ankle on
the day of the Trials finals and watch thousands upon thousands
of hours of planning and dreaming painfully dissolve. In the sport
of track and field one cannot be right every day; what is important is to be great on the right day.

In months past, before the accident, Heidi's whole life had
been directed toward this one day. There can be no certainty that
he would have made the team. However, on the day he was
injured he was a finely tuned machine capable of clipping off
four-minute miles regularly, and he would have had three more
months to become as fit as possible for the Trials. In March of
1976 he was in a group of American 1,500-meter runners that
was separated by the barest psychological thread. Then, instead
of running, he had to watch the 1,500 final on television.

It began with a searing pace. The first 800 meters went in
1:51.3 and it blew away the stragglers. Among them was Mike
Durkin, Heidi's old foe, who was tempted to drop out in the first
400 meters. "I was in last place and trying to improve my position
and I'm saying to myself if this is a sixty-second pace I'm going
to have to step off the track because I can't pass anyone," commented Durkin afterward. Obviously, he had misjudged the
pace, which was hotter than sixty seconds. He knew he could
come to life in the last 400 meters when strength means every-

thing. Durkin steadily moved up through the bunched pack and then, while the other runners were falling to pieces, he began his sprint, his lift.

The bell clanged for the last lap as Durkin put on the pressure. The Hayward Field crowd jumped to their feet, their cheers rolling into the infield.

The runners hit the backstretch, a time of pain and concentration. Durkin felt great. They rounded the top of the final turn. Durkin had more left. He was with the leaders, shoulder to shoulder, and his legs were so light and relaxed that he felt he could run forever. He wasn't even conscious of his arms pumping. Reaching. Reaching. The cheers drove him on. He was hanging on . . . hanging on . . . And then, suddenly, it was over. The arms and legs of runners all swarming over the finish line. Durkin eased up near the tape and finished third. He was trembling. Something had enabled him to run 3:36.7, the equivalent of a 3:54 mile.

Incredibly, he had trained for only ten weeks. Before he began to train he had not given the Olympics serious thought. His time of 58.4 in the last 400 meters had put him on the team. Ken Popejoy was eighth in the nine-man field in 3:53.9 and he ended his competitive career on that day. Durkin had caught everyone, including himself, off guard and only his sheer jubilation exceeded his astonishment. "God, I can't believe it!" he cried. "I went to church this morning and prayed my head off. Praise the Lord! He put power in my legs. I feel like doing cartwheels . . . !"

In Bloomington, Heidenreich did not share Durkin's joy. He had watched Rick Wohlhuter, an Olympian at Munich in 1972 and often a rival of his, win the race at Eugene. He had watched Matt Centrowitz of the University of Oregon place second. Heidi had beaten Centrowitz before.

However, none of this failed to break Heidi's spirit. His mother had for many days sensed his need to get on with it: "He was itchy to get back to Bloomington, to get it moving again. It was like his first day at home . . . 'Okay, I'm on my feet. Let's go . . .' Every day it was let's do something more. Still, I don't think he ever realized how much he yet had to do, how long a time it was going to take him to recover. I wondered if we would have to take him to a psychiatrist when he first came home, not knowing what his reaction would be to the Olympic disappointments."

DeLoris Heidenreich settled in her own mind how her son passed through those summer months, saying:

". . . I think that God, in His way, kept him little while he needed to be little so that he did not realize what all was going on."

Steve Heidenreich reentered Bloomington Hospital on July 8, 1976, for a cranialplasty, the insertion of a stainless-steel-mesh reinforced plastic plate in his skull where Dr. Rak had sawed out the bone for the craniotomy in March.

Heidi's memory mechanisms still were not functioning. He did not remember the doctor, although he did recall one or two of the nurses. He was discharged on the 13th, sooner than Dr. Rak had anticipated. Steve was pestering the doctor with a request to go sailing. Rak squelched this idea and many others that required physical exertion. Patience was not a Steve Heidenreich virtue.

The doctor did give him some advice. "If you are ever in a gun fight, turn your head to the right," he said, laughingly explaining to Heidi that the right side of his head was now as strong as steel. A small caliber bullet could not pierce his new plate—only ping it and leave him with a memorable headache. The doctor also warned him not to expect that he could now step into a telephone booth and emerge with a giant "S" on his chest, able to leap the Penguin malt shop in a single bound or dash a 3:58 mile.

Heidi's parents had traveled to Bloomington to help him move into his room at the Regester, a house that had served as a shelter, a port of call, for IU track and field athletes for more than a decade.

After his parents left, Heidi's days were occupied with the Olympic Games, which he watched in the evenings at Beth's apartment on her TV.

Heidi saw nine world records established at Montreal. The American men won six gold medals and on a comparison basis of the first six finishers in all the events they led handily. He was astounded at the awesome, protean achievements of Finland's Lasse Viren, who scored a double by winning both the 5,000 meters and the 10,000 meters, a repeat of his outstanding performance at Munich in 1972. No runner before, not Paavo Nurmi or Emil Zatopek, had won the two events in successive Olympics. A rumor flew through the Olympic Village, where the athletes were housed, that Viren's proficiency was attributable to blood doping, an experimental process whereby some of an athlete's blood is withdrawn and the oxygen-carrying hemoglobin is extracted and stored. When the athlete's body has regenerated the absent red blood cells the hemoglobin is restored, giving the runner more than he had naturally. Theoretically his system then has a larger capacity for carrying oxygen to the muscles. At Montreal Viren denied, but rather coyly, the rumors that he did such a thing.

The 1,500, Heidi's race, was the event upon which he turned much of his concentration. It was not an exceptional final but this was understandable since the preliminary heats had sapped the runners of their strength.

In all prior Olympics only five runners had done under 3:40 in the heats. At Montreal there were twenty-five who ran that fast. One was Mike Durkin, who clocked a 3:38.0 but did not make the final. He later discovered, to his dismay, that he had become the fastest non-qualifier in history.

Walker had run 3:36.9 in his heat, extremely fast for the preliminaries. In the final Walker lingered in the pack until three laps had been completed; then he launched his sprint. His kick nearly betrayed him in the last fifty meters. In his weariness his pace slowed. His reckless expenditure of energy had worn him out and bound his muscles in tight bunches. But he had enough left to blunt the bids of everyone behind him in a maelstrom finish and he won in 3:39.17, the slowest Olympic 1,500 final in twenty years. Finishing fifth was England's Frank Clement in 3:-39.7. Heidenreich had beaten him at the World University Games in Rome in 1975.

Encouraged by the brisk racing he had watched for a week at the Olympics, Heidenreich stepped up the distances of his daily walks and slow jogs in anticipation of the return to hard workouts that Dr. Rak had okayed for August.

Time. Everything good takes time. The rain had stopped on the morning of August 29, and now as Steve tightened the laces of his training flats there was a hint of nervous expectancy in his deliberate movements. This was the day that it started for him, the day that regimented, regular workouts began again. The rain had done nothing more than thicken the air, and the humidity, as it can be on an August day in southern Indiana, was oppressive. Sweltering.

Never again would Heidi run at night. His training pattern had changed to morning and afternoon workouts. He had jogged once after dark since the accident and it had frightened him. Running on the sidewalk instead of on the road was confining, as well.

On August 29 Heidi ran slowly for four miles but it was far enough to empty his mind and when he got into the fourth mile he was in a trance. In the beginning his legs were wobbly, but when he had moved farther on he felt better. For an instant he was spurred by a fierce pride and he pushed the pace a little, his shoulders erect, his head up, and his eyes set on a line ahead of him and not gazing at the road where his footfall was forming a pattern.

When he ran, whether it was a scorching sprint on the backstretch or an easy jog, his linear, elongated frame fit a perfect form. A deer, Beth Burnside had called him. Graceful and smooth. As the humidity closed about him his lean body glistened with perspiration and soon he was water-splashed and his orange Adidas running shorts were soaked. His steps were light and bouncy until he swung north on Indiana Avenue and as he began an incline at Dunn Meadow his arms and shoulders stiffened with fatigue. He hurdled a carpet of leaves that had been caught up in a swirl of water that morning and were soaked and matted alongside the curbing.

With a few hundred yards left in his run he felt a sharp pain in his legs. This was a familiar warning signal and it is the bane of runners who are not fit or who begin to run again after a prolonged absence. It was shin splints, a dull ache that is the result of inflammation of the muscles along the tibia in the lower leg. Shin splints commonly occur from running on hard surfaces. Treatment can be ice, heat, taping, aspirin, arch supports or rest. Heidi chose rest after running four days with the pain and with blisters that had developed. He took a week off and tried it again. No pain.

The setback annoyed him because frozen in his memory was the ineffaceable joy of how it was before, running free and easy. But he knew he could work at it. Everything good takes time.

That autumn of 1976 was as difficult as the months of July and August had been, fraught with barricades that seemed to be stopping him at every turn. After he had accepted the reality of the accident, his resentment and bitterness steadily grew and manifested themselves in his immaturity and sarcasm and waspish moods. He was disillusioned and confused and deeply frustrated. "I don't think any of us knew half the problems he was having then," his mother said later. "People looked at him and thought that because he was up and walking around that he must be perfect again. They didn't realize how far he had to go. Beth was good for him. She kept him going and she encouraged him and praised him. She scolded him, too, when he needed to be scolded."

Beth had postponed her career so that she could stay in Bloomington to be with him in what was, essentially, a mother-son relationship. She was working during the day. She prepared supper for him every evening. Many of his days were spent in her apartment where he was waiting for her when she returned home from work. On one such evening, after Beth had prepared a sumptuous meal, they were sitting on the sofa, not saying anything, their eyes locked together dreamily. He took her hands in his.

"Steve," she murmured.

". . . Please."

He put his arms around her. They kissed.

". . . Please stay tonight."

They reached out for each other, touching. Steve pressed his lips against her brown hair. He turned out the lights.

From that night they practically lived together. In the fall, after his classes began, she was with him every night, either at his apartment or the Union or the library while he studied. She read and wrote letters or helped him if he got stuck on a word or could not phrase a sentence with the proper meaning. He began carrying a dictionary with him everywhere in case a word eluded him in the midst of a conversation. "I was there to give him strength," comments Beth. "I always tried to be positive but it is not easy to be that way all the time unless you remind yourself. If he complained I pointed out the good. He needed to maintain his perspective."

Which was becoming more and more difficult to do. Steve experienced a devastating blow to his confidence in a business course when he innocently asked what a balance sheet was and the class roared with laughter before they realized and stopped themselves. Equally as degrading was his inability to run with the freshmen on the IU cross-country team—he was too slow to stay with them. The will was there but the speed and strength were not. Most of the endurance he had built like layers during nine years and thousands of miles of training was gone.

He went to Sam Bell, shattered, morose and in emotional turmoil.

"Coach," he said, with panic in his voice. "It's not there anymore. I'm running ten-minute miles. Those guys . . . those freshmen, are making me look like a piece of you know what. What am I going to do?"

Bell looked at Heidi silently. For a few moments neither spoke. Bell was torn by the same emotions that had brought Heidi to his office in despair. He shook his head.

The coach stood. Slipping an arm around his athlete's shoulders he said: "Steve, why don't you just go off and run by yourself. At your pace. The hurt won't be nearly as great as it is now; the hurt that *I'm* feeling for you now, too."

Like most runners, Heidi kept a diary. In it he recorded the number of miles he ran each day, his nagging pains, the quintessence of his day. His diary became his heartbeat.

His entry for September 11 noted:

It took me an hour to run about seven miles. Need to rest.

On September 12 he wrote:

Accumulated mileage for week was sixty-seven. Doesn't seem like I have gone anywhere. I guess it will take a while.

Even so, he was running. First he had to win in his race against himself. He had sneered at the odds before, why not again? Heidi's real strength during the autumn of his rebirth was his giant ego which he tapped often. "I believed that it wouldn't take long and all those freshmen—everyone—would be seeing my back and my heels again," he says.

"I was running by myself. Heck, almost anybody could have kept up with me. I was told I had permanent brain damage. I was told that school would be hard but that I could handle it. I was dumb enough to believe them. It made me want to do supergood work just to show everybody. But I couldn't. Not yet. Sometimes I would sit for twenty minutes trying to think of one word."

In the months that followed, Heidenreich's out-of-control emotional inconsistencies and his roommates' refusal to accept these locked in an impasse. Eventually they ruptured the friendship. Heidi's bitterness did not abate—he felt betrayed. He threw himself into his running and his classes because they mattered immensely to him. He wanted to prove to himself that he could lift himself, in both, back to his level before the accident. There was a marked change in Steve Heidenreich. No longer was he a man of conviviality. No more did he go bar-hopping. He could not.

Beer, the water of life for distance runners, was forever off limits. The accident had destroyed many of his brain cells and abstinence could help preserve those that remained. Heidi concurred, reluctantly, with the doctor's ruling.

More than anything else, his roommates at the Regester missed the Heidi they had known. The old Heidi and the good times. After a number of difficult arguments, Steve Weiss leveled with his roommate. "We want to give you all the chances you need," he said. "But it's sad, Heidi. You're like a machine. Your routine every day when you come home from class is the same. You don't talk. You go up the stairs . . . clomp, clomp, clomp. Slam your door and we never see you again."

Beth could feel the crackling tension. She was a part of it. "It wasn't that Steve did not care for them anymore and if they had been willing to sit with him at the library every night he would have been fine," she said. "They wanted to go out drinking. He couldn't. He looked to me for companionship. One of his roommates told me he hated me. My blood went cold. Steve was told he was spending too much time with me. He defended himself by saying, 'Don't you normally spend a lot of time with the person you're going to marry?' "

Ultimately, it came to a summit session. Steve Weiss and Mike (Doc) Dutchman and Steve Heidenreich met over dinner. They thought him capricious and insufferably aloof. He thought them insensitive and truculent.

"Look," said Heidi with an unsettling glance, "you don't know what I've been through. You say I've changed. How? Put it in writing. I want to read it."

Within days he was given a formally written explanation. It read:

We want you to move out simply because our lifestyles are so different. It seems you have put tremendous pressure upon yourself to succeed in track and academics. But you have forgotten to leave time for your friends. We feel uncomfortable around you. It is because you are so serious and introverted. You've often said 'you don't understand.' If you would just open up and tell us about your problems we would come to understand you better. What hurt most deeply is when you told us that nothing mattered more than Steve Heidenreich. All of your time had to be channeled into regaining your intellect and your physical strength. We know that you can't go out and drink beers with us. But a wall has been built between us. It is difficult to ask you to leave, which is only a polite phrase for kicking you out. We hope you succeed in all endeavors. More importantly, we hope you realize how valuable your social life is.

Sincerely yours,
Michael F. Dutchman

Bewildered, Heidenreich sent the following memo to Tom Berry, his attorney, and to Dr. Rak: "Apparently my personality has changed because of the accident. My former roommates, who were two of my best friends, asked me to leave the apartment. It seems I've become self-centered."

Brain-lobe damage can lead to an accentuation of a person's traits of personality. If a person was quiet before, as Heidi was, he can become very withdrawn and rigid, developing fears and phobias. When Heidi's frustrations reached the boiling point he entertained the notion of quitting school. Dr. Rak then sent him to Patrick Utz, the staff psychologist in the Counseling and Psychological Services at Indiana University. Utz probed the contingencies of Heidi's changes through interviews and tests and discovered from them that Heidi's anxieties—his loss of memory, his distractibility, his reading deficiencies—were being multiplied in his own mind in great part because he was a runner. He was aware of his body and its limitations much more than a nonrunner would be.

A runner listens to his body, perhaps more than does an athlete in any other sport. If there is pain the runner will back off from the stresses of violent workouts until the pain is located. His body is sending him warning signals. Likewise, a runner will know, after a period of years, what kind and how much training he needs—the combination—to achieve the hairline balance that encourages steady improvement and discourages fatigue. The runner aims for the balance when he can run increasingly longer distances without a great increase in effort. This is the essence of running, the pleasure that it offers. From the fun comes a good feeling and from the good feeling comes a desire to continue.

Heidenreich's changes, the accentuation of his traits, were not uncommon for one whose brain lobes were not functioning properly. "There was a complicating factor, however," says Utz. "Steve had his life kind of planned out. Everything was going to happen at a certain point and that was gone now. It put him at a crossroads." There were two separate strains in his character. One said go; the other raised self-doubts.

At this point in his life he would have knocked down any wall to achieve a goal that he had set for himself. This intensity undoubtedly did more to speed the healing process than anything else. But what would happen to him if he could not achieve a really difficult goal, whether it was the 1980 Olympics or the 1984 Olympics? Steve had realized quite early in his life that he wanted to be a runner. He was looking for identification. Running was more than what he did. It *was* Steve Heidenreich, his very being.

There never was one specific moment when Heidenreich decided to continue his interrupted chase for a place on the United States Olympic team. Beth, for one, was prescient. She knew he would all along.

If Montreal had been taken from him he knew there was Moscow in 1980. And if not Moscow, there was Los Angeles in 1984. When he was socked by the realization that running back was not going to be anything but sheer, unmitigated sweat and toil combined with a lot of luck, he moved his goal up about twenty notches and became obsessed with reaching it.

It made him giddy to think about maneuvering himself toward inclusion among the world's running elite again. One night, after Steve and Beth returned from the library, she asked him what it was that drove a runner with the necessary talent to try and become an Olympian. The idea absorbed her; she could not understand the sacrifice.

"Why do you want it so bad?" she asked, a quizzical smile on her face.

"I want to succeed," he said promptly. "I want to become the best runner I can. If that takes me to the Olympics . . . well, great. You can be a successful athlete and still not make that team. You get one chance very four years, so a guy has three, maybe four, chances at the most to ever get to the Olympics. I won't have even that many."

"Uh . . . look, I don't want to misjudge you," she said. "I understand what you want to prove to yourself. But . . . uh, what can all this do to a marriage?"

Heidenreich stared at her, his face tense and aggressive. "Beth, I'm telling you what I am. I'm a runner. I want to become the best I can. I want to travel. If I can do all that and marriage doesn't interfere, fine. I am what I am."

Beth laughed woodenly, a little shaken. "You're crazy in the head, Steve Heidenreich."

He shook his head. "No. One of the best, that's what I want to be again. They took it from me. Nothing will stand in my way now. Okay? You've gotta be tough, Beth. Hard-core. No B-e-e-e-s, no G-e-e-e-s."

As the autumn leaves scuttled in gusts of wind, the healing of Steve Heidenreich inched along. He remained almost reclusive. Winter came. Problems he was having with his classes remained more intractable than he ever could have imagined. But some of the stabs of desperation that he had suffered from were softening. There were hints of the old Heidenreich. His parents saw a reawakening of his sensitivity in a letter from him. "Good things have come from this accident," he wrote. "I'm closer to people."

He had for some time been planning to surprise Beth, having bought a diamond ring. He'd been waiting for the right moment to give it to her.

One Saturday evening in late January was particularly frigid. The thermometer had plunged and the announcer on the car radio said it would be below zero by morning.

Steve and Beth returned to her apartment from dinner at a restaurant near the College Mall. They laughed as they scampered from the car to the door and squeezed into the room together, anxious to let the warmth touch them. Once inside, Beth quickly hugged Steve and kissed him hard.

"Hey!" he said. "What's that for?"

"For taking me out tonight. It was neat."

Beth was bubbling over with high spirits. She gazed at him with blue eyes that embraced him. Her chestnut hair shone in the soft light.

"Steve."

"Hmmmmmm?" He was taking off his coat.

"Do you think it was predestined that we met?"

He smiled. "How would I know?"

"Well, it was a coincidence, remember. I mean, that we both decided to go to summer school. There were so many things that could have prevented either of us from going."

"I suppose . . ."

"No, seriously! It happened so quickly and easily."

"What?"

"What . . .!" She rolled her eyes toward the heavens.

"You sat in that chair in front of me and I decided you were pretty darn cute."

"I know . . . I know, and I thought your legs were terrific."

In the next moment the world stopped for both of them. In that moment Steve made their engagement official. He slipped the ring on her finger. She was in his arms in an instant, quivering with excitement. She could feel her pulse pounding in her throat.

"Steve! Oh . . . Steve!"

They kissed tenderly, surely.

While Beth sat on the floor he plucked a guitar and sang to her from "Venus and Mars," the Paul McCartney song that had filled the room with its steady beat on the night that he had returned from Russia and they had slow danced, swaying to the music.

The act of putting a ring on Beth's hand did not signal great changes in either of their lives. Steve, in fact, was badly in need of a transfusion of confidence. The entry in his running diary for January 30 was this:

Workout—I ran well considering the snow I had to run through. Comments—I must start getting some intensive long road runs in and start developing my legs in weight lifting. I must get intense.

The entry for February 8 was this:

Workout—Indoor track. Warmup. Two 660s in 1:45 with a 30-second rest between each. Two 660s in 1:45 with a 15-second rest between each. I felt tired. I felt sorry for myself.

Heidi's daily routine during that spring of 1977 left little time for social life. He only saw Beth when she sat with him while he studied. His impatience was building. He wanted to regain everything that the accident had taken from his running. Immediately. Or by tomorrow at the latest!

For a while he was running three times a day—morning, noon, and late afternoon. He had a course at the business school from 3:30 to 4:15. He took to wearing his running clothes to class so that he would not waste a minute. As soon as the class was over he left his books at the Beta Theta Pi house nearby and off he loped for a four-mile run. He got back to the fraternity in time for his job washing dishes. By six o'clock he had returned to his apartment and had taken a shower. Then he studied for the rest of the evening.

His weekly mileage was fluctuating between sixty-five and eighty miles. His studying and classes required ten hours a day, including the time he spent with tutors at night. Because his ability to reason was impaired, the amount of time he had to spend on his studying was tripled.

To evaluate the complexity and depth of his impairments Heidenreich was tested at the university's Speech and Hearing Center. His reading skills were found to be severely limited for one of his age. When he was given instructions to "pick up the green square and touch the white circle" he could not remember the specifics of the directions. When he was asked to restate an abstract paragraph on the value of life, he could not. "It's over my head," he said.

His incapacity to reason logically wound him tight as a clock. Yet he refused to accept less than what he thought he was capable of achieving. All of his anger, frustration, and his feelings of self-deprecation couldn't even begin to match his determination. He vowed to those who tested him:

". . . I can do it. I'll get better and I'll come back and pass your test with flying colors. You watch me. I'm going to show you that people can come back from a serious injury and do anything they want. Everything that was taken from me I'm going to get back. You watch!"

Steve took IQ tests in the autumn of 1976 and again during the summer of 1977. "Already in 1976 he was talking of graduating from IU, of the possibility of graduate school and of Moscow," says Patrick Utz, who supervised the testing. "On the repeat test his score had jumped by ten points. The important thing about this is that more than one year after the accident he was continuing to show significant progress. If 100 percent is the goal, he is close to that. The rest of his improvement will be fractional. However, the difference between again being a world-class runner and just good could be fractional."

The gap is infinitesimal and almost imperceptible. But it is there.

11

April 1 broke with a bold sun and azure sky. It was on this day that Steve Heidenreich made his return to competitive racing. He did it in such a manner that it refreshed flagging memories. He did it so that the whole world would know that dreams—his dreams—die hard. His training had gradually been increased in its intensity and his progress had been unusual.

Heidi ran 1,500 meters on the IU track in an all-comers meet. The meet was open to anyone who cared to run, and few did. It was an informal and relaxed afternoon of track and field before an audience of only a few persons who happened to wander by, unaware probably of the one-act drama that shortly was to un-fold. The fourteen runners in the 1,500 were from the Indiana team and the Indiana Track Club.

The coach, Sam Bell, laid a hand on Heidi's shoulder.

"Go out slow," he told him. "Don't push yourself."

Heidi nodded.

"The race is against yourself," said Bell. "Your only opponent is you."

At the starting line, in lane four, Heidi yawned nervously.

"Gun's up!" someone shouted. The starter, in position, fired. Cr-rack!

The runners bolted. In spite of his jagged running skills, Heidi did not labor. Bell commented on the progress of the race for a

147

television station that taped the event. As the pack hurried through the first lap the coach talked to himself and to Heidi in the microphone, not loud enough for his runner to hear.

"Oh, that's nice," observed Bell quietly. "So nice . . . be smooth . . ."

His stride unchanging, his motion fluid, he was running easy and relaxed and without fatigue. He ran so softly that there was no slapping sound when his spiked shoes struck the artificial, red-tinted surface of the track.

"Think pace," continued Bell, the verbal link between coach and runner empathetic more than real.

Heidi suddenly accelerated sharply and swung wide to shoot around two runners and go into fourth place. There he stayed. Three runners in front of him were so far ahead that the gap was insurmountable, even for one who was in a stalking position and whose spirits had been lifted by the smallish spurt.

"Smart move. Smart! . . .

"Pick it up now . . .

"Arm action. Use the arms . . .!

"We want four minutes. Don't regress."

But he did. The goal of four minutes was unreachable. For now. Regardless, Heidi was running with no discomfort and he was so relaxed that his jaw was bouncing. He had known this marvelous feeling intimately and often at a much faster pace, on other days, before the accident. Today it was irresistible. It was a nurturer of hope.

The hands of the watch passed four minutes before he could step across the finish line. He was fourth in 4:02.0. Tom Burleson won the race in 3:53.8.

Heidi won *his* race. It was an enormous victory for him, a virtuoso performance. On March 25, 1976, he had to be lifted into a chair because he could not straighten his debilitated legs. Three hundred and seventy-one days later he ran 1,500 meters in 4:02.0, the equivalent of a 4:19 mile. This was a miracle—in anybody's book.

Heidenreich wanted no pats on the back, however. After he jogged an easy cooldown mile he walked to where his sweats lay.

As he stooped to pick them up, rivulets of perspiration dripping from the tip of his nose, he reminded a friend that his time was some twenty-four seconds slower than his lifetime best. "Now I know where my needs are," he said. "Weight work and hill work. I need strength. But I had nothing to lose. If I had done poorly what difference would it have made? From as far back as I have to come?"

More difficulty was on the way. Beth had changed jobs. She was working in a bank at Columbus, a city thirty-three miles east of Bloomington. The ties between Beth and Steve had gradually loosened in the months of March and April. In May when Heidi graduated she returned the diamond he had given her.

"He was trying to turn me into an athlete and I was trying to turn him into a socialite," says Beth. "He wasn't a regular at plays and I dragged him to those. He didn't enjoy them. We were both trying to make each other our perfect person . . . which wasn't working out."

Beth had begun to date others when she moved to Columbus.

"I have discovered a life of my own," she told Steve. "You want someone who is an athlete. We're not suited in that way. You need to prove to yourself, and to me, that you can live without me. I don't want you to be that dependent on me."

Heidi accepted her decision. He felt hurt but upon reflection he decided she might be right. To make it back as a runner and as a whole person he had to do it alone. His love for Beth did not diminish, though. They were going their separate ways for now but neither was completely sure if they wanted to break it off forever. Their fondness for each other could know a renewal when Steve was better.

He finally had his degree, bachelor of science in business administration. This was a milestone, a giant step forward in his comeback; he had beaten the odds again. He had raised his grades from D's in the autumn of 1976 to B's with admirable diligence. His cumulative grade point for four years was 2.95, just shy of a B average. In a few days he was to begin a full-time job at the IU Credit Union. As a finance major, he calculated that his world wasn't spinning too badly.

At Nick's he slid into a booth with a friend. The waiter handed him a menu and asked, "Will you have a drink, sir?"

"Sure," said Heidi. "A Seven-Up."

He grinned at his friend. "Invent me a beer that will grow brain cells," he said.

It happened on May 20, a Friday. Steve Heidenreich was riding his bicycle on Indiana Avenue and was just beginning to pick up speed down a small hill when a university-owned van shot through a stop sign.

"Ooooohhhh!" said Heidi to himself, remorsefully, "I'm going to hit you soooooooo hard!"

And he did. He jerked the bike to the right but it was not enough. Bike, Heidi and van collided. His left shoulder struck the door on the van's passenger side and the left side of his head smacked the window, cracking it.

His feet locked in the toe clips, Heidi and the bike lay in a heap in the street. Slowly, he attempted to untangle himself.

The van's driver, Joseph Amundson of Bloomington, looked at the squirming cyclist. "Oh, my God . . . don't move," he said. Another motorist who had witnessed the accident called police on his CB radio.

Soon, an ambulance pulled up and Heidi was en route, again, to Bloomington Hospital, where he was X-rayed. His head was okay; his shoulder was not—he had suffered a minor separation.

A Bloomington orthopedist, Dr. Sterling Doster, examined Heidi further and explained that a lump on his shoulder would be a lifelong reminder of the mishap unless he cared to have it removed surgically. He was also told that the lump would be a minor nuisance if he wanted to skip surgery.

His decision was easy.

"No thanks," said Heidi. "I'm tired of operations. I'll take the lump. See ya."

The doctor mailed the results of his examination to Heidi's neurosurgeon, Richard Rak, and attached an addendum. "This young man's luck never seems to change," he said.

Heidi did not wish to risk losing a single day of running because of surgery, which would have put his left arm in a sling. His shoulder bothered him the rest of the summer but he ignored the twinges of pain. He had to stop lifting weights for a while but he ran the day after the collision.

By the end of June his training was going well. He wrote in his diary: "I'm starting to get settled down and my confidence is developing. I should do well in the Freedom Run."

This was a six-mile race that was held each July Fourth in Bloomington. The first and last miles were flat, the middle four hilly and unforgiving. Heidi had run eighty-seven miles, ninety-nine miles and ninety-five miles in each of the three previous weeks in preparation for the race. Five days before the race he ate vegetables, fruits, and nuts and on the next four days he went on a juice-and-water fast.

He asked his parents to come and watch the race. On July 3 he ran with his dad and noted in his diary that he felt relaxed. "Tomorrow should be a good race," he wrote.

Race day was hot and humid. Heidi did his stretching exercises and jogged a mile warmup. The first mile of the race was too fast for him with an under-five-minutes pace. As the runners hit the first of the hills he throttled back some and tried to run relaxed. He worked his way up from twentieth place to third going into the fourth mile and held the position. The runner in second place, Tom Burleson, was far ahead and that was how they finished. Burleson's time was 31:49. Heidi, placing third, ran 32:06. He was overjoyed.

To him this was the first solid confirmation that his running might again approach a high level. "I was surprised to run six miles that well against fairly good competition," says Heidenreich. "It was real good for my head. I was thinking, 'Wow, I've still got a long ways to go but as well as I'm running now think what I'll be running next year. Just great!' Everything was starting to go my way."

After the race he was ravenous. He had taken nothing other than liquid for four days and realized now that juice diets were not wise for him. The race had begun at 11:00 A.M. and the sun and humidity had combined to drain his strength. He went to the first ice cream store he could find and ate a pint of frozen yogurt. That night, before he went to bed, he wrote in his diary:

I took a big step today. It has boosted my confidence. I ran a great race. I should have tried to catch Tom Burleson.

Steve Heidenreich was running back.

Even Sam Bell and Dr. Rak were astounded that he was running so well, and they had both been exposed to his unyielding determination. Heidi was reminded of his superb races at Kiev and Prague in 1975. But he did not feel that he had reached the pinnacle of his career then. The satisfaction of that journey would never be enough to last a lifetime. Not for him, anyway. "I want to do it again," he said emphatically. "I think I can." The hunger to win.

How far he could go, Dr. Rak estimated, would be decided by how hungry he was. "Generally speaking, with brain injuries virtually all improvement is made within one year," says the doctor. "He had continued to improve beyond that period. At the time of the accident I was fairly certain that he had no motor impairment and that he could run again because it is an automatic function. A runner does not have to remind himself continually to move his feet. What distinguishes a runner from someone who is a world-class or consistent winner is that which is deeper: the desire and ambition and compulsiveness.

"I thought he'd be able to run again but I did not feel he could ever again be able to race or be competitive. He is and this is beyond what any doctor would expect by any stretch of the imagination."

Early in 1975 a group of twenty world-class American runners were brought to the Institute for Aerobics Research in Dallas for a series of psychological and physiological tests that might give a decipherable pattern of why one runner is faster than another. They wanted explanations for the fact that certain runners dominate distance races, and sought to determine why the tissue, biochemistry, cells, and fibers of one runner's muscles allow him to be faster or more enduring than another.

One of the tests was performed on a treadmill. The runners

breathed into a mouthpiece that carried their breath to a row of bags. They ran at different paces and at increasing grades, the treadmill steepening in slope by two and one-half percent every two minutes. The test determined oxygen consumption during maximum stress per kilogram of body mass per minute.

By measuring how much oxygen is being taken up, the difference between the inhalation and the exhalation, the potential of a runner's oxygen pathways—the heart, lungs, and blood vessels—can be estimated. Usually, but not always, the percentage is an index of a distance runner's abilities. Theoretically, at least, the higher the maximal reading the better the runner should be.

The late Steve Prefontaine was one of those tested at Dallas. His oxygen uptake was 84.4, one of the highest ever recorded in a runner. The average for the other runners was 76.9. The average for a jogger is between 46.0 and 50.0. Frank Shorter's reading was 71.2 and yet his three-mile and six-mile times were almost identical to those of Prefontaine. Why? It is thought that the best marathon runners (the event in which Shorter won a gold medal at Munich) use less oxygen than runners in shorter events. However, the answers are not so easily categorized. Some marathoners apparently can run farther and faster on the amount of oxygen they consume because of a chemical reaction of muscle cells. Or it may be because they run efficiently, with a style that does not require as much energy.

Heidenreich was similarly tested at IU in 1976, soon after he had run a four-minute mile indoors. His oxygen uptake was 72.0. He was retested in August of 1977, twenty months after the accident. The reading had plummeted to 68.0. A reduction can be expected when a runner is inactive for a year or more, but a world-class runner can, with adequate training, regain previous readings even after inactivity.

Heidi was apprehensive. Following his second test he feared that his skills might be irretrievable. It was explained to him that a drop to 68 was significant but not nearly as drastic as might have been expected, considering the trauma his body had gone through. His anaerobic capacity, however, was tremendously reduced. In other words, he was not taking in enough oxygen under stress to meet his body's needs.

"When you run your muscles contract," Sam Bell explained to him. "They get their fuel, their energy, from glycogen that is stored in muscle tissue. The glycogen is formed from glucose, a natural sugar, which is carried in your blood. As long as the glycogen levels stay high, muscles can keep functioning at a steady pace. When the glycogen supply is depleted, the muscles slow or stop working. You become fatigued and your performance is inhibited.

"When you are fit you are able to perform efficiently in a steady state. This means that your body is functioning aerobically. It is able to transport enough oxygen to the parts of the body that need it. As you become very fit your blood flows through your lungs in a greater supply and your body can extract more oxygen. The larger your oxygen capacity, the longer you can run at high speeds without becoming fatigued.

"But when you cannot breathe in enough oxygen to take care of the body's needs you become anaerobic. Your body is in oxygen debt and it obtains the energy it has to have by converting glycogen into lactic acid without the use of oxygen. Lactic acid in the bloodstream, even a tiny amount of it, is enough to retard the ability of your muscles to contract. As the acid builds in the blood you feel muscular pain. There is a limit to how much oxygen debt your body can tolerate before you slow down or stop. And when you do stop you are breathing hard. This is how you repay the oxygen debt. Your body accomplishes this by converting the lactic acid back into glycogen.

"Blood carries away the wastes from your muscles. Your blood is mostly water. As you run your muscles heat up and you perspire. This is nature's air-conditioning system. As the fluids are lost your body tells you that they need to be replaced and you become thirsty."

Heidenreich interrupted. "What you are telling me," he said, "is that by increasing the supply of glycogen in the muscles I could run for longer distances without as much discomfort. Right?"

"Exactly," said Bell.

Heidi's brow furrowed. "How?"

"One way is by eating carbohydrates. The body converts them into glucose. This isn't so important for races of 1,500 meters or 5,000 meters. You can develop your ability to withstand fatigue by training anaerobically. This you have to do by interval training."

Heidi quickly glanced at Bell. "Will it take long?" he asked. "I don't have much time. The 1980 Olympics are just around the corner."

Bell laughed. "You're not patient, Steve," he said. "But you can be excused for that. World-class athletes wouldn't be world-class if they were patient. You are going to need a minimum of two years of hard training to return you to the level you were at. The changes in your performances will probably come slowly. You will get discouraged. Unfortunately there is no way we can predict how fast you will improve.

"Biochemically, world-class runners are similar. The difference comes in the runner who is able to obtain the most from the capacity he has. Physical factors are only partially responsible in dividing the best from the others in a group of gifted runners. Desire is important. Consistent high-level performances are probably ten percent mechanics and physiological and ninety percent psychological."

Heidenreich had fought through nearly every barrier that the world of medicine associates with total recuperation from brain damage. Could he do the same with his running to again be among the world's elite before the United States Olympic Trials in the summer of 1980?

He was as impetuous as ever. As he left Bell's office and started for his car to go to see Beth in Columbus, he felt replenished. Although the romance between Steve and Beth had cooled, it was by no means over. They had put it on hold. Beth continued to date others but Steve did not. His running was his social outlet. It absorbed him.

To Beth, running was abstruse. "It wasn't enjoyable," she says. "I just don't like to run. Steve always told me it is a natural thing. I was in awe of him and this drive that he had. I could never figure out what the appeal of running is. He loved to teach me how to run and he made me run with him. I'd run three miles and fall down in the grass out of breath and he'd come and pull me up. He was very patient with me. 'C'mon . . . C'mon,' he'd say, 'you can do it.' "

They took a picnic lunch to a park near Columbus. Late that afternoon, before returning to Beth's apartment, Steve ran gently on some trails in the park and coaxed Beth to join him.

"It's enjoyable if you work yourself up to the place where it isn't fatiguing," he said. He talked to her as they jogged.

"Just relax. Hang loose."

"Let your foot hit the ground flat. Breathe through your mouth and your nose with a nice, even rhythm. Hold your arms like you're resting them about waist-high and don't swing them hard. That uses up your energy.

"Relax. Think about relaxation. Convince yourself that you're a rag doll, so relaxed that you feel like you're limp. Don't clench your hands or your teeth. That tightens the muscles and the tightness will soon pass to your shoulders, your arms and to your legs.

"Press the top of your tongue lightly against your lower teeth and let your jaw flop. Check your forehead. Don't frown. See how loose you are?"

Heidi arose early the next morning to run five miles at a golf course in Columbus. Beth did not run with him. Even the instruction of such a fine teacher was not as appealing as an extra hour of sleep.

Running for many Americans is linked to their school yard memories and the belief that it is only pain, torture, and agony. Few physical education instructors teach that running can be a pleasurable and healthful avocation that can be followed for a lifetime.

A decade ago runners out on the roads were considered peculiar, but in a few short years, road running in America has become the popular outlet for the jogger and the elite runner who attempts the marathon.

For most runners the marathon is not a race, it is a personal experience. It offers the change of scenery, the rolling of the hills, the minor challenges that one does not find on the track. The track can be boring and pressurized. The runner on the track is a spectacle, not a free spirit. In a marathon the runner goes through many physiological changes and moods. He learns to cope with all those different stressful situations—the heat, gravel, pavement, grass. This is the impelling challenge that heightens a runner's self-esteem and enhances his meaning and being.

Running forges a peace with man's inner awareness. A runner smells the grass, feels the twigs crackling underfoot in the autumn or hears a soft rain pelt the leaves. At that moment a runner can imagine himself to be a hawk wheeling in a blue sky.

When fatigue is absent, running feels good. But the runner should not expect this glow to be a constant state. There are days when running is difficult and there is discomfort. On those good days, however, running can free the mind of nervous tension, irritability, and feelings of panic, and the runner can identify with nature and merge with it. Running can be creative if the stop-watch is put away in a drawer and the runner goes easily and feels no compunction to catch the runner in front of him and compete with him. Competition can come later when the runner is fit, and only if he wishes to compete. The runner should pick routes that offer different scenery, different terrain—a park, a road, a forest, a beach, a mountain. Running enhances the quality of life. Anyone who stays with it for a year will be hooked. No one is ever the same again. Running produces tranquility.

Chemical changes in the brain, perhaps in the limbic system where emotions are generated, are thought to produce the serenity or high that a runner experiences. The high is a state of total relaxation and quiescence that may last for hours after the run is completed.

For Heidenreich, a morning six-mile run is a release. He lets his mind float; he daydreams; he sings silently to himself. If he is running alone he will surge with strong bursts whenever he feels like it. "Running is an outlet for me," he says. "I don't know what I would do if I could not run. Running is fun. I can't believe how much work people make out of it. It should be like play. Like fun and games. Like getting away from the office."

And invigorating. "When I'm running I feel more alert," says Heidenreich. "Often if I was studying for finals late I went out for a run rather than drink coffee to stay awake. I feel better in the morning after a run than if I sleep in. Often it is a mind game. I prefer to run in warm weather. Muscles can relax in cold weather but I make it a chore to let them. I say to myself, 'Muscles . . . you'll be tight,' and they are. I hate to run in rain. I'd rather run in snow or when it is thirty below. The worst is having to crawl out of bed in the morning when it is thirty-three degrees and raining. But on a warm day after a long run the feeling I get is indescribable. I just want to shout, 'Ahhhhhhhhhhhh! I feel great!' "

Running without fatigue can free the brain, allowing the runner to ease into a sensation of euphoria. Regular running for periods of up to an hour can produce the kind of pleasure that runners learn to crave.

Peter Strudwick, a California schoolteacher, embodies the self-esteem that running provides. He was born without feet, without a right hand and he has only two fingers on his left hand. His mother had German measles during pregnancy and his handicaps are congenital.

As he slowly plodded up the incline of the street toward the finish of a marathon in a Midwestern city he was preceded by police motorcycles. A man with a bullhorn proudly announced: "Here comes Peter! Here comes Peter!" A mass of runners, spectators and meet officials scrambled to find a place so they could watch. As Strudwick stepped across the finish line sirens screamed and spectators cheered and pounded each other on the back. One woman wept.

He was in last place. He needed almost five hours to run the course but his time was immaterial. He runs on the stumps of his legs and wears no shoes when he runs. He has no toes. He coats his sweatsocks with a silicone-rubberized material. When it dries it forms a hard substance that can withstand the pounding on the streets. He slips the socks over his stumps and holds them in place with rubber bands when he trains daily and runs in races.

"Running is such a ridiculous thing for me when you think about it," says Strudwick. "I'm always last. But I get my rewards. Health; the friendships I form. Running makes me proud. As long as I am going to have problems in life I may as well meet them head-on."

Heidenreich's morning runs and his workouts are separate but his mind controls both. "I do the work to get my body, which takes about ten percent of my effort, ready for races," he says. "The other ninety percent is in the mind.

"Running is an art. How can I use my mind to become the best performer that I can? Performing is the same whether it is running, music, or business. It's all a mind game. My morning runs are relaxed, an escape.

"But practice is intense. I don't daydream while running in practice. It doesn't do me any good to dream about the future. I must be so concerned with the present that I have the best practice I can. My mind tells my body to relax. It's just like putting yourself under hypnosis. Some days in training you feel like you can surpass anything you have ever done. It's like going into another world."

This is also one way that Heidenreich deals with prolonged pain when running hard. "I'll disassociate the pain," explains Heidi, "but only if the pain is such that it will hurt my performance. I'll think about something else, anything to keep my mind off the pain. I prefer to keep in touch with my body at all times. To read it; to feel it; to adjust to the warnings if it is being overtaxed. The only fear I have with disassociation in workouts is that I might let my mind slip too far away from me and trip off into the twilight zone."

Disassociation is a kind of self-hypnosis that reduces the discomfort. Many marathoners adopt this when they "hit the wall" at twenty miles, that invisible barrier that can put the mind through the severest test an athlete can know. It is at this point when breakdowns often occur in the body. Glycogen supplies are depleted, there is a loss of blood volume, body temperatures rise, and the body becomes dehydrated.

Inuring oneself to pain is an art learned by practice. Elite marathoners assert that if they're feeling bad they try to push harder because they know the other guy may be worse off and may let go. The ability to organize oneself to maintain his discipline and concentration is a mental dimension that sets a runner apart. It is controlling every move to a specific end so that there are no lapses, so that the mind is not going a hundred different directions at once.

Form is important because an extra inch of knee lift translates to three inches of stride, and over twenty-six miles that can be a lost of wasted energy. Runners must constantly be aware of armswing and of relaxation in the lower back and in the foot plant. The more they are attentive to these details the better they become.

Above all, the runner seeks economy of movement and in a marathon he constantly monitors the runners around him. He pays attention to their breathing and after a while he knows exactly how they feel. If they stumble he knows it. If they begin to breathe heavily he knows it.

The Dallas study found that elite runners performed at seventy percent of their aerobic power when running at ten miles an hour, compared with nonelite runners who ran at eighty percent of their maximum. The elite runner's cardiovascular system is so superior that he expends less energy during a race than the non-elite runner.

The trick is relaxation. An athlete goes out with a preconceived notion of what he wants to do on that day. As much as possible he wants to have things his way. The more they are, the easier it is to relax.

In America, athletes are not equal. The professional is eulogized by traditionalists as the only true athlete. But is the runner who averages 4:50 a mile for twenty-six miles any less an athlete than, say, basketball's Julius Erving, football's O. J. Simpson or baseball's Reggie Jackson? Not at all. The difference is by what criteria an athlete is recognized by the American sports fan and the media. Interestingly enough, as running becomes a vogue, the athletes of other sports are coming to the disciplined runner and asking, "How do you do it?" There is envy of the runner's mystique. They want a piece of it.

The traits that distinguish distance runners from other athletes are aggressiveness, introversion, and obsessiveness. They turn their aggression upon themselves as a means of motivation. But runners are at the top end of the scale in emotional stability. By their willingness to test their bodies and their minds, you shall know them.

And by a runner's food intake shall he establish his individualism.

Heidenreich does not rely on a special diet to improve his running. He watches his weight. Extra pounds can only impede a runner's efficiency. He avoids red meats, preferring instead fish and fowl since red meats are more difficult for the body to digest. He eats fresh fruit, vegetables, and salads. These foods meet the nutritional needs of any runner without special food supplements or vitamins. He does not practice fasting.

For runs of more than an hour a high carbohydrate diet can double the glycogen content of a runner's muscles and increase his endurance. However, the extra glycogen also triples the water content and can produce a feeling of stiffness in muscles. Carbohydrate loading is accomplished by depleting the body's glycogen supplies one week before a race with a long run. For the next three days foods high in fat and protein are taken in. The last three days the runner mainly eats foods high in carbohydrates.

For a runner, nutrition of the mind comes after that of the body. The workouts and training, the motion itself, give a runner something to look forward to. A runner never wants to retire, does not want to be done. The runner wants the freedom of forever being able to jog five miles one day and three miles the next day, at his own pace, detached, in his own way, reaping the rewards. Very few people have that power over themselves. A runner has.

12

The autumn of 1977 was a period of restlessness for Heidenreich. He struggled with the impairments that profoundly affected him and his running. Before the accident Heidi took his running gifts for granted. Now he doubted his ability, and the unshakable confidence he had always exuded was gone. His full-time job at the IU Credit Union depressed him because it was consuming more hours than he wanted to give, hours that he felt he should be devoting to his running.

Beth did not agree with him about the job and the division of his time, and they argued often. Many things irritated him now —a rebellion had begun to stir within him. Even getting up in the morning sometimes seemed impossible, especially when the weather was bad. When his roommate Tom Tepley called his name at 6:30 on a rainy morning he swore under his breath. Why was Tepley always so punctual?

As Heidi lay unmoving he could feel the dampness. He could hear the rain tapping on the side of the building and he cursed his rotten luck. Without looking out the window he knew the morning was bleak and gloomy, and that his morning run was going to be a joyless chore. It seemed he could hear a faraway voice entreating him to go back to bed. Running could wait. Lazily, he fell face-first onto the bed and buried his head in his pillow.

Only a few minutes later he felt a tugging at his ankle. It was Tepley.

"Hey, c'mon man. We gotta go . . ."

Tepley was from Cleveland, Ohio, a genial guy with a perpetual smile. He also had an uncanny ability to pull out of the past vivid descriptions of Heidenreich's waggish adventures when he was a junior and senior at IU, and Heidi liked to be reminded of those days.

The two-bedroom apartment, identical to the others in the vast complex that was built around a swimming pool, served as a temporary home but little else. The decor, a curious mixture of styles, was strictly functional. A dingy brown sofa and chair with herniated springs were the only formal pieces of furniture. The indoor aerial on the TV set had been fashioned from a coat hanger. In the living room stood a bookcase filled not with books but with Heidi's medals and souvenirs from his trip to Europe in 1975. The walls were decorated with pictures of Olympians. Scattered on the living room floor were copies of *Track & Field* and *Runner's World*. The refrigerator shelves were always crammed with plastic gallon bottles of water and little else. When the four apartment dwellers returned from their runs, all they wanted was to quench their thirst and as quickly as possible.

Heidenreich finished dressing, walked into the living room and sat on the rug. As was their custom, Tepley held his legs while he did sit-ups and then they did some stretching exercises together before leaving the apartment.

The day was awful. Heidi had the feeling that all of his strength had been drained from him by the hour and the weather. But once outside, he pulled the hood of his rain jacket over his head and thought about the run ahead of him, and his blood began to flow swiftly. He could feel all the parts of his body waking. His neck. His shoulders. His arms. His legs.

Silently, they ran together on the soaked streets. They were unmindful of the faces in the cars that turned to look at them quizzically as they passed. Their steps took them down the twisting asphalt grade into Cascades Park and along a tree-lined stream.

Heidi wiped the moisture from his face and gulped in air. Running was his fortress, a wall behind which he could retreat. It gave him a sense of protection and was a cherished possession that, he felt, belonged only to him.

Heidi relinquished the shower to Tepley when they returned, and sat down at the kitchen table to make an entry in his diary. He wrote slowly and stopped. He winced. The word he wanted was not within his grasp. In a flash of fury he jumped up and hurried to the living room, returning with a dictionary.

"Help me," he said to Tepley, who had finished his shower and was standing at the kitchen door.

"Sure. But you've got to tell me at least part of the word," said Tepley.

"Uncer . . . uncert . . ." He shook his head in disgust.

"Uncertainty?" asked Tepley.

Heidi's eyes twinkled. "That's it," he said. "Boy, am I a dummy. One of these days I'll learn."

He wrote in his diary:

It seems like some of my problem is psychological. I have been trying to defeat myself. I must watch my weight and get ready to fight. My head is not together. Work has really burned me out. Uncertainty clouds my future.

He was attending a reading improvement class at the university, and each night he practiced his reading for one hour with a storybook written for fifth-graders that he had checked out of the Monroe County library. His textbooks were practically unfathomable, and whenever he attempted to absorb any of the information they contained he generally stopped after half an hour of frustrating work, rested, and then began again.

He was plagued with reminders of the accident. One of them was his eyesight, which had worsened. "I'm blind as a bat now," he said to Tepley one morning. "My contacts are okay, but I'll never wear glasses again. The ones I'd need would be as thick as Coke bottles."

Heidi had placed his college diploma on a dresser near his bed. It also was reminder, a reaffirmation of what he had been able to accomplish. He looked at it daily. It quickened his pulse, it inflated his confidence and it made him feel like a scholar.

Despite the tangible proof of what he had achieved, the reminders of the accident seemed increasingly difficult for him. They were like a malignancy that spreads insidiously. He did his best to push them below his consciousness but he could not shake the sense of emptiness and a feeling that his future had no dimension.

One evening, alone in the apartment, he was overwhelmed with the meaning of what had happened to him. He remembered himself before the accident, thoughts of his past flooding his memory. The tears welled up and he pounded his fist against a wall at the inconsistencies of fate. He wept, convulsive sobs shaking him. Why him? What would happen to him? Would he ever be the same Steve Heidenreich again?

His mind was numb. His rage spent, he put his head down on his pillow and slept dreamlessly.

The breach between Steve and Beth continued to grow wider. She had her friends and he had his. The changes in Steve and his new immaturity, however temporary it might be, made Beth doubt that the relationship had any real future. Somehow, they didn't have much to talk about. She was willing to overlook many of the difficulties, but the disparities between them were too great. They were reluctant to admit that the romance was over, though it seemed to have been doomed from the moment that Steve was hit. Nothing had been the same since. They were both ambivalent about splitting, however.

They had not seen each other for some time when Beth called one night and found Steve to be very cool toward her. He had interpreted the period of her silence to be her desire to break away completely, and he did not want that. But whenever they had tried to talk of a possible wedding date, they ended up skirting the issue because they could not agree on what part of the country they would live in and because they could not resolve several other differences. To avoid a blowup, they just avoided the issues. All they were doing, though, was putting off a final decision. But Beth had finally concluded that she really wanted to be engaged. It was, she thought, a status symbol of sorts. And it would still give them time to think about the wedding.

Within the span of one twenty-four hour period they argued and decided to end it. Then, as if to assuage their feelings of guilt, they became engaged again. Steve gave Beth a single rose to commemorate their reconciliation. She was overjoyed by the gesture—the gift meant more to her than a ring. She placed the flower in a vase and did not touch it until the leaves had dried and turned brown and crumbly.

In late autumn, Steve ran well in cross-country races at Notre Dame and at the University of Wisconsin-Parkside at Kenosha, representing the Indiana Track Club in both races.

He refused to permit feelings of weakness to invade his daily life. He had to prove his courage, his strength. This was part of his obsession. He wrote in his diary of a workout in November:

> Ran eight miles slowly. It was snowing and cold. I was a puss today. I didn't want it. I became discouraged. I need to act like a champion every day. I need to be tough inside. If I want to go as far as I can I have to live running. Work was a pain in the butt today. I have to learn to keep my job and running separate and get intense in both.

On November 26 Steve ran in the AAU national cross-country race at Houston, a meet open to anyone. It attracts many of the top collegians and often some current American Olympians, as well as postcollegiate distance runners who aspire to be Olympians, and some of the foreign runners who are studying at American universities. This mix provides a strong field. The courses on which the races are held are almost always demanding and difficult, and can grind down the strongest of runners.

Steve wrote of the race in his diary:

> I went out as planned. My first mile was 4:45. Unfortunately I was so far behind at a mile and a half that when the going got tough through the ditches I felt sorry for myself, as did everyone else around me, and I did not aggressively attack the flat areas to try

and catch those ahead of me. Next year I must go out fast the first mile with the leaders and then settle into a relaxed rhythm so I will be close enough to make the kill when the opportunity comes.

The next morning, after his return to Bloomington, Steve and Tom Burleson ran thirteen miles on a snow-packed road that made footing treacherous. In the afternoon, Heidi went cross-country skiing for two hours. That night his groin muscles were sore and for the next few days he could not run because of inflammation in his Achilles tendons. These injuries, which hit him with no warning and stayed with him for a full month, were due in part to his zeal. They interrupted his training and made him irritable. He had pushed himself too far and his body had rebelled.

In December, Steve and Beth agreed to call off their engagement for good. They had been clinging to the hope, faint though it was, that their relationship would work out. Beth, uncertain of how to put her feelings into words, finally told Steve that he needed her more than she needed him. He was too defensive to allow himself to admit openly any personal hurt and so he used his visions of greatness as a buffer and, superficially, his bravado covered up his misery. Reflecting about the past few months he wrote:

> It appears that I've made the year a disaster. My groin hasn't healed yet because I lack the patience to let it. Beth and I are just friends now. Our relationship has been like a yo-yo this year. It's nice to get the uncertainty over with, however I must admit that I'm hurt and lonely. My intuition tells me Beth is lonely too. Being independent should be good for me. This way I'll take control of all variables controlling my success or failure. Since I've not been pleased with the way I'm performing I feel sorry for myself. Sad to say this but basically it is my fault. From now on I'm a champion. Every day I'll work at becoming great.

Beth accepted the split more philosophically than did Steve. "We probably should never have gotten engaged at all," she said later. "At the time it was wrong for both of us. The only bitterness that I feel is in what the accident took from Steve and the damage he suffered and what *he* had to go through. All the hopes and dreams he had were shattered."

He had seemed so unreal to her in the aftermath of the accident. How different their lives together had been before—the real life, the incandescent days she remembered so fondly. She looked back wistfully, knowing she always would wonder what the future might have held for them.

January 1978.

It began to snow at eight o'clock that morning in Bloomington and a wind came up and blew the snow into drifts. Few cars were moving after an hour or two. Not much of anything or anybody was moving. It was so cold that it hurt the lungs to breathe in the air, and Heidenreich actually skipped his morning run. At ten o'clock, bundled up, he stepped outside into the bitter cold for a walk. He had a decision to reach. He stepped carefully through the snow, his leather boots leaving deep footprints. He mulled over the problem again: his job at the IU Credit Union. He wanted more time to run and he was being denied it by the management. Which came first, his job or his running?

Day by day he had been fighting a desire to quit. His confusion mounted until he decided what he had known all along: His running came before his job. He resigned.

He had to sell his Volkswagen Rabbit because he could not meet the weekly payment, but soon he found a part-time job as a salesman at a store that specialized in running shoes and athletic wear. He existed on the meager salary of $45 a week, just enough to pay his share of the rent and the food. It was worth it because he had all the time he wanted to train. His dad asked on the phone one night if the store where he now worked was close enough that he could walk to it. "Walk!" he exclaimed. "Who walks? I run!"

Steve had been on his new job for only a few days when he met a young woman who came to the store to buy jogging shoes —Connie Gingery. She was a graduate student in music at IU, a soprano. As she left the store they agreed to meet the next night. She drove over and picked Steve up when he finished work, and they went to Nick's, where they found a quiet table in the back. For two hours they exchanged small talk, going through the what-do-you-like and what-don't-you-like routine and swapping bits of family background. Nothing deep, each self-consciously trying not to say anything dumb.

She was different from Beth, he thought. He didn't always trust his first impressions but he knew from the outset that she was far quieter and perhaps not as businesslike. He felt relaxed with her. She told Steve that she recognized him when she entered the store, and that was certainly flattering! She had been working at the university student loan office when he had stopped in to pick up an application the previous year, and another girl in the office had told her that he was Steve Heidenreich, runner.

Connie was really into athletics—running and racquetball. Steve thought he was extraordinarily lucky. They talked and laughed that evening until late into the night. Within days they felt comfortable around each other. He picked her up after her classes one afternoon and went with her while she vocalized in a practice room at the school of music. Connie was petite, five feet tall, with dark hair, perfectly proportioned, delicate features, and a wonderful smile. It amazed Steve that someone so small could belt out such a powerful sound when she sang.

"You're a runner, you should understand," she said, chiding him. "It's in the breathing." Heidi laughed heartily and agreed that it must be the same.

They ran together on one of their first dates. She charged up the hills, pumping her arms furiously, much to Steve's delight. He liked a competitive partner when he ran. At times she was quiet with him, at others she bubbled over with laughter and charm. She was energetic, an excellent athlete—a perfect companion for Steve.

The next week she invited him to meet her on the racquetball court where she promptly handed him two lopsided defeats. They ate dinner that night at Connie's apartment and the next day they ran three easy miles, talking as they ran. Their runs together turned out to be a good way to get to know each other.

The two began seeing each other with increasing frequency.

Steve caught himself coaching her, reminding her that she could not develop her voice potential unless she adopted a positive focus and kept it. His own attitude about himself and his potential improved. Connie, like Steve, was aggressive, a high achiever. She had graduated from IU with distinction. Early in their relationship he saw that she was strong and determined. She fit snugly into Steve's concept of what he was searching for in a close friend: one who was intelligent and a good listener and who could handle his moods; one who would be solicitous of his obsession for running. Her devotion gave him reassurance and his enthusiasm never failed to delight her. They soon realized that with each other they had a sense of well-being and that they loved each other very much. Two months after they met, Steve knew he couldn't do without Connie. He wrote:

> We've been spending practically every minute together. We have been keeping each other up late talking about everything, every subject imaginable. She has a special type of beauty in her personality. She is so loving and tender and interesting. We will learn what it is like to live with each other on a daily basis.

On March 16, two years after the day of the accident, Steve wrote:

> In the morning I ran the Sorority Road Run. It was five miles and it felt good but I need to get out of bed earlier to have more time between workouts. In the afternoon I ran at a good clip for six miles when I became fatigued. But I kept it together. I cooled down and ran to work. An excellent day of training. Living with Connie is helping to improve my outlook toward life and toward training. I'm much happier now.

Late in March Steve and Connie made plans to drive to Florida for a vacation with Tom Burleson and his wife. They had already left Bloomington and were to wait for the other couple in Fort Lauderdale. The Florida sun seemed enormously inviting as they ran together through falling snow in Bloomington on the morning of the day they left. The snow continued to fall throughout the day and into the evening. They finished packing and left in Connie's tan Pinto at nine o'clock, driving east to Columbus, Indiana, and then south on I-65. "Florida is going to be great," Steve said as he drove. "I can hardly wait to soak up those rays."

Interstate 65 stretched due south toward Louisville, Kentucky, like a roller-coaster strip of cement through the hilly countryside sometimes called the "Hoosier Alps." Near Seymour, Indiana, the hills were glazed with ice and mirror-smooth.

Deceiving, how normal and safe they appeared, Steve thought. The trucks were rocketing onward, many whipping past him, their headlights bouncing as they rolled by. He could see the drivers talking on their CBs. As Steve and Connie neared Seymour he pushed hard on the accelerator and the car swung left to pass a semi that suddenly had slowed. As Steve shot into the left lane he saw what the trucker had seen: an oil transport, dead ahead, jackknifed across both lanes.

Steve wrestled with the steering wheel and stabbed at the brakes. He could not turn right because the truck he had passed blocked the way. He could not turn left because the driver of the jackknifed transport was tramping toward him in the snow on the edge of the median. Neither Steve nor Connie spoke. Through the windshield they could both see disaster in front of them. It seemed to be happening in slow motion. Steve punched the brakes with his foot but the ice kept him from stopping; the car careened on, its wheels locked, sliding on the ice, and both of them were certain they were going to die in a few seconds. They watched the horror about to happen.

Then came the impact. The little Pinto slammed under the oil transport. There was the crunch of metal against metal and the sound of shattering windshield glass filled the night air. A steel tool box on the underside of the transport caught the Pinto's roof and peeled it back.

Steve broke the silence. Connie heard him gasp:

". . . Christ! . . . Get out! Get out! . . . It might explode!"

They opened the car doors and fled. Connie slipped on the ice and fell but quickly picked herself up and stumbled to reach safety. The driver of the truck they had passed summoned police on his CB as the traffic behind them, stopped, began to stack up.

Soon Steve and Connie were sitting in an Indiana highway patrolman's car and he asked if they wanted to go to a hospital. Both demurred bravely but Steve could feel a lump forming on the right side of his head above his metal plate. Connie, trembling with fright, bit down on a sliver of glass that had worked its way into her mouth. She felt her face. There were pieces of glass in her hair and she thought she felt a sharp object in her left eye. The patrolman called for an ambulance.

Half an hour later, they were being examined in the emergency room of the Jackson County Memorial Hospital in Seymour. Connie was okay. Steve's skull was X-rayed and a nurse later showed them the pictures of the mesh steel plate. "It's a real masterpiece," Steve said to Connie as they studied it.

The two were shaken but otherwise all right. Nevertheless, they stayed at the hospital that night. Steve's sleep was fretful and he awoke once, perspiration covering his face.

At 7:00 A.M., Connie came to Steve's room and shook him gently. He awakened and turned eagerly to her, feeling instantly relieved at the sight of Connie's face. They kissed. His arms enfolded her and they clung to each other fiercely as they relived the nightmarish, chilling moments of the previous night.

Their elation at being alive was like a high, but they were uneasy about traveling so soon after the accident and checked into a motel where they stayed until the following morning. Florida seemed a million miles away. The white sand of the beaches and the misty spray of the huge waves flying in their faces at high tide seemed to be little more than an illusion when compared to the reality of the moment.

The next day they rented a car and returned to Bloomington, all thoughts of the trip tabled for at least a while. Late in the afternoon they ran three miles together on one of the university's indoor tracks and that evening they celebrated their exceptional good fortune by visiting one of the town's finer restaurants.

Connie had known Steve only a few months but during that brief time she had come to appreciate his indomitable will and how he seemed to be driven by an inner gale of energy. Sitting across the table from him as they dined, she gazed into his eyes.

What was there about this man, she wondered, who could be vibrant or sullen, who could run like lightning or sit unmoving, speak or be silent, laugh, weep, love, dream, be blithe or bitter? What was there about his proclivity for death?

"I don't understand it, Steve," Connie whispered. "It's spooky. Are there cosmic implications? Are you being tested by some force? Is it some curse? Either you are one of God's chosen people or you were born with a black cloud over your head."

Heidi shrugged. His spirituality was not something he talked a lot about. He had been reared in a home devoted to the worship of God and, since the accident, he prayed each morning during his run. Like Connie he wondered, too, about the meaning of everything that had occurred.

"Am I being tested?" he said, repeating her question and pondering his luck.

"I don't know if it's God or not. I don't have mystical insights. I don't worry about it; I won't change my life-style. I'm still running out on the roads and I cannot be any more cautious than I am. I was cautious before. What can I do when I'm riding a bicycle and a guy runs a stop sign?

"I keep riding the bike. I still drive a car and I still run. I have no fear of these things. I have no fear of death. Why should I fear it?" Connie shook her head and said nothing. There was no way she could question his acceptance of these things. His faith was intact; it was deepened and enriched. He was not fatalistic; he wanted to fulfill the best of himself.

In April, Heidi prepared for the Dogwood Relays at the University of Tennessee, a meet that he felt was a crucial gauge of his progress. He was to run 1,500 meters in an invitational race. A week before the meet he did one particularly intensive day of training. In the morning he sprinted the hills of Dunn Street. In the afternoon he ran 400 meters in 61.9 seconds, 800 meters in 2:07, 400 meters in 63.4 and four 150-meter dashes as fast as he could. To end the workout he lifted weights and then ran to work. It had been a seventeen-mile day and he still felt fresh at the end of it.

On race day, Heidi, representing the Indiana Track Club, lined up with the rest of the field. He stood timidly, his eyes downcast, his arms hanging limply at his side. Tom Burleson watched from the side of the track.

"I would have given anything to somehow light a fire under him," said Burleson later on. "There were runners that he had creamed before the accident; some were standing around him and they didn't even recognize him." Heidi didn't look up as he stood at the line, alone. Some of the other runners had never met Steve; others who knew of his accident would have had difficulty believing he was running at this level so soon.

Four years earlier, when Steve was regularly crushing the competition, he had on this same Tennessee track won the mile in 4:02.3, then a Dogwood Relays record, and later in the same afternoon had come back to anchor IU's four-mile relay team to victory with a 4:03.2 mile. Burleson shook his head sadly. "Man, if you guys only knew now how he was then," said Burleson under his breath as the gun sounded and the race got underway.

Heidi knew he was in trouble immediately. The pace on the first lap was very hot and it discouraged him. He scarcely had time to feel sorry for himself, though. As the runners rounded the second turn on the opening lap someone fell and the runners behind him, in domino fashion, stumbled and went down. Steve avoided a calamity by swinging wide, all the way out to the eighth lane, but at that instant his race had come apart at the seams. When he had freed himself of the traffic jam the leaders were long gone and he was alone, running in last place. The fallen runners had quit.

Stung by the unexpected pileup, he lost his concentration and his vigilant will. He finished in 4:08—a 4:25 mile—and he angrily removed his spikes and threw them at the ground. He started for the IU team bus and found that the door was locked.

"Hit the door with your head," Burleson laughingly suggested to Heidi, trying to revive his spirits. "With that metal plate maybe you can spring the door."

Heidi smiled weakly. He didn't really appreciate the joke. On the bus ride back to Bloomington he discussed the race with Sam Bell.

"You know, Steve," said Bell, "I don't think you would have beaten the world today even if *no* one had fallen. But you probably would have been around 3:55 and that's thirteen seconds faster than you ran. I know you're discouraged, but the one thing you are going to have to have if you want to succeed is patience. It's going to take time."

Steve, stammering with anger, smacked his fist against his hand. He absolutely could not abide failure. But his pride, his single greatest motivation, got in the way.

"Patience . . . !" he snarled, his combativeness flaring. "Patience! What the hell . . . I've been running since last fall!"

Bell reminded him that the groin injury he had suffered back in November had cost him valuable days of training. "You need miles, Heidi," continued the coach. "You have many miles to go. You must build a solid foundation and that takes time."

That night, before turning off the lamp by the side of his bed, Heidi wrote:

> 4:08. How embarrassing. I felt like a Little Leaguer trying to play in the majors.

The next morning, a Sunday, Heidenreich dutifully arose and ran, although it was not easy for him. The desire to quit was growing ever stronger. It permeated his thoughts and feelings. On the road through Cascades Park he saw only the solitary figure on the track at Knoxville, alone and in last place and falling farther and farther behind. It was as if part of his body was being lifted and transported to another time and another place. When he became dispirited, which wasn't often, he permitted himself the option of quitting. How easy it would be to walk away from the fight, remembering what he had and what he had achieved. This did nothing more than provide him a momentary release, however, for he knew beyond any doubt that he had taken solemn, sacred vows that he could not break. Not ever.

13

Steve Heidenreich will be twenty-seven in 1980, an age that will not preclude his dream of a spot on the United States Olympic team if he can regain the fitness and the racing sharpness he possessed in 1976 before the accident.

He knows his body faces the supreme challenge and that certain healing processes cannot be artificially speeded up. He knows, too, that his best chances of making the team are probably not in the 1,500. He will have to move up to the 5,000, an event that does not require the constant competitive racing and track workouts to stay sharp, and allows a runner the freedom and flexibility to do more of his training out on the roads. This new possibility fits Heidi's needs perfectly anyway. This is how he can rebuild his base, the foundation that was taken from him by the accident. The atrophying of his body was deleterious because it stripped him of his strength. In a desperate attempt to regain strength as quickly as he could—strength that usually is more critical to a miler than to a 5,000-meter or a 10,000-meter runner—he changed his diet, eating large amounts of foods high in protein, and stepped up his weight-lifting exercises.

Everything that he lost in the accident will have to be regained by natural means, and it can be in time. A sound diet is essential. But what he needs most is time for nature to take its course. More and more frequently there are moments of exultation. Two days after the run that had infuriated him, he ran ten miles with the IU team on a hilly, demanding course. He started slowly and caught everyone but Tom Burleson, finishing with a time of 51:24. It was his fastest ever for the course. After the long run he wobbled through the front door of his apartment, shoes in hand, his legs stiff and aching. He was walking on his heels because of two large, ugly blisters. He slumped into the old brown chair in the living room and sighed. "It just goes to show you what your head can do for you," he said, reacting to the unexpected results of the day, a day to savor.

Distance running requires purity of purpose. It is a contest against oneself, not so much against outside forces. When Heidi was a member of the Indiana team he rarely ran ten-mile distances, instead doing shorter interval workouts on the track. Heidi has a sense of himself, his limits, his goals. The sharp edge of his drive is as keen as it ever was, and he is perfectly prepared to struggle with a new and different training program.

Some of his skills are not what they used to be, but more important, perhaps, is his aggressiveness. He is running and clutching at a dream and living his dream twenty-four hours a day. His goal, the 1980 Olympic team, may seem unreachable, and how much of what he can regain of what he had before is uncertain. His chances, he figures, could be the same as those given him after the accident of being alive today—about five percent. But no one expected him to live, either. And, as he has said, "The Olympics are important but they are not the only race. I want to become as good a runner as I can again. That would be super. I'm still young and I still have time."

Dr. Rak knew that the odds against Heidenreich ever racing again competitively or succeeding academically at a college level were overwhelming. When Steve did race again and did graduate the doctor was then asked the logical question: How much of the damage is irreparable? It is a question with which any neurosurgeon has difficulty, as the innermost secrets of the brain are rarely revealed. "I don't know if he has permanent impairment," says Dr. Rak. "I am sure there is something missing. He is not the same person he was before. Even though his recovery was extremely rapid—probably because he has more determination than any patient I have ever had—I'm sure there is something different about him. He is not the same but he is close . . . close but not perfect."

Those who endure great pain sometimes acquire gentleness. Steve was beginning to see a different purpose for himself through his running. On May 22, 1978, he wrote:

> I feel that I'm not doing anything with my life. I've got to get it in my head that I'm a leader who can set an example for many people. One who can inspire them to reach high goals.

He was encouraged in this by Chet Jastremski, a Bloomington physician who had walked the very path that Heidenreich is now attempting to follow. Jastremski, a swimmer, had changed the basic concept of the breaststroke—revolutionized it, actually. In one magnificent August week in 1961 he smashed all four listed world breaststroke records.

His own success had not been easily achieved. Before 1961 and in the years that followed he endured many disappointments. His frustrations began in 1956 when, as a fifteen-year-old from Toledo, Ohio, he was disqualified at the Olympic Trials because an official ruled that he had executed an improper turn, kicking one leg six inches deeper than the other. In 1960, then a member of IU's swimming team, he was left off the Olympic squad when, inexplicably, the selectors chose to fill only two of the three spaces on the team available for breaststrokers. In 1964 he won a bronze medal at the Games in Tokyo. In 1968, then twenty-seven, he went to the Games at Mexico City as an alternate, but did not get to swim. At thirty-one he tried, and failed, to make the team for the Games at Munich.

Jastremski advised Heidenreich not to fret over the time he had lost from competition, telling him: "Physiologically, there is no reason why a person could not swim better at thirty-one than at twenty-three. Swimming, like running, is ninety percent psycho-

Running Back **179**

logical. It is a matter of building mental barriers and then breaking them. In theory, endurance also improves with age."

Heidi's soul and his spirit will be the pivotal factors in his chase for the stars. They will either reward or deny him the consummation he seeks in life. "He has to think he will be able to do it," says Dr. Jastremski. "If he does, everyone around him will too. If they don't, he won't. Desire makes people do things better than they ordinarily would. As long as there is something in sight we really, really try. For Heidenreich the 1976 Olympic Games were close. He could smell them; he could almost touch them. Steve still has to climb to the top. He knows he can. In all respects, he should not be alive today. But he is and he is running and it is a miracle. His recovery and what he has accomplished is one in a million, probably."

Beads of dew still hung heavily on the grass and shafts of the early morning sun filtered through the trees on the large wooded lots of Heritage Woods, a quiet enclave of expensive homes on Bloomington's outskirts. Tom Berry stood in front of the bathroom mirror, his face covered with shaving cream, listening to a radio announcer's monotone voice recite the events of the world that had occurred while he slept.

He had just applied the razor to his chin when his wife, Sue, appeared in the doorway holding the morning edition of the Louisville *Courier-Journal.* She stuck the paper in front of him and the thick, black letters of the headline seemed to leap off the page.

MYSTERY WOMAN CLOUDS HEIDENREICH
HIT-AND-RUN CASE

Berry's eyes quickly dropped to the lead paragraph of the story.

BLOOMINGTON, Ind.—In a bizarre twist that rivals a Perry Mason plot, an unidentified woman has turned up as the possible driver of a vehicle that may have struck former Indiana University track star Steve Heidenreich on March 16, 1976.

". . . What?" exclaimed Berry. "I'll be damned . . ."

A towel draped over his shoulder, he pattered down the stairs to the den, wiped the lather away from his ear, and dialed the home number of Edward Eckert, the Monroe County prosecutor.

"Ed. Tom Berry here. Sorry to bother you at home but I've got the paper and there's a long story on a new development in the Heidenreich situation. What can you tell me?"

Eckert was thoughtful. "Not much," he said. "David Colman phoned me yesterday and said one of his clients had told him that his girlfriend had admitted responsibility for hitting Heidenreich. But Colman won't identify either one of them. I'm willing to offer the girl immunity from criminal prosecution if she'll come forward and tell us what she knows."

Berry wondered about this for a moment.

"What do you think, Ed?"

"I think we'd better get to work on it."

"Sounds good. I'll be in touch."

David Colman was a Bloomington lawyer whose practice was primarily criminal defense. He refused to divulge the names of the suspects because to do so would violate privileged client-attorney confidentiality. He was not, however, involved legally either with Steve Heidenreich or Sonny Thorsrud.

Colman's position was not popular among his fellow barristers in Bloomington. He was an aggressive young attorney who wore Levis and a leather hat, instead of the pin-striped, three-piece suits of his profession. "The local lawyers have given me the SOB award," he once said. "I'm the villain. But it is a matter of principle with me. I don't want to be a martyr or a scoundrel. The expedient thing for me to do, I guess, is to answer the questions."

Which was exactly what he was going to have to do when Don Robertson, Sonny Thorsrud's attorney, petitioned the Lawrence Circuit Court in Bedford for a hearing.

Judge Glenn Stieg, after listening to testimony, ruled that Colman should be deposed and, if asked to do so, reveal the names. Facing a contempt citation, Colman refused to budge. What followed was a complex series of cat-and-mouse legal proceedings as Robertson took his appeal to the Indiana Supreme Court to force Colman to disclose the names. The appeal was denied.

Berry, dubious of Colman's motives, was walking out of the courtroom when Roger Finders, a Monroe County deputy sheriff, fell into step beside him. "I'd be willing to bet a bundle that Colman's man, the one he won't identify, is Reggie Parker," said Finders.

Berry stopped abruptly. Finders seemed convinced. "Think so?" said Berry. "Let's find out."

Reggie Parker was at that moment in the state reformatory at Pendleton, Indiana, Finders told Berry. He had been convicted of fatally stabbing a man on a street in downtown Bloomington. Colman was Parker's attorney.

On a hunch, Berry drove to Pendleton. Parker was not there. He had been transferred to a minimum security prison at Rockville, Indiana. In the office of Warden Richard Sanders at Pendleton, Berry searched Parker's packet, a file of personal information that is compiled on each prisoner and includes a record of all those who visit him.

He flipped through fifty pages of Parker's life history and between the fifty-first and fifty-second pages he found what he was looking for, a card which had stuck to one of the pages. On it were the dates of visits from Colman and from one Kim Randle.

Berry smiled broadly. "See this," he said to Sanders enthusiastically, pointing to Kim Randle's name on the card. "She was here to see him every week . . . !"

His appetite whetted, Berry left Pendleton and drove immediately to Rockville, where Parker was brought in handcuffed. Berry was certain that he was about to uncloak the mystery woman.

"Who's Kim Randle?" The lawyer asked.

"My fiancée," answered Parker.

"Where is she now?"

"In Indianapolis. She lives there; we were living together. She's got a job there at a women's exercise salon."

Parker then poured out his story. He was desperate, he said. He was in a state of depression and he wanted to test Colman's loyalties, hoping, he said, that Colman would tell police about a mystery woman and that the ensuing publicity might force a new trial for him.

Berry stopped him. "This is all so illogical," he said. Berry was jotting notes on a pad. He put down his pen.

Parker's face reddened. "After I talked about this with Colman he said he wanted to do something about it immediately and I told him to wait, that I was lying about Kim and to forget about it."

Berry scribbled hurriedly. "Did you have any other girl friends at the time you were talking to David Colman . . . other than Kim Randle?" he asked.

"She's my fiancée, man. I had lots of girl friends."

Parker had learned details of the Heidenreich accident from the newspapers, he said. He added that he had talked often of the accident with the prisoner he worked next to in the prison hospital. This was Paul Cox, a twenty-six-year-old meat cutter whose criminal career had been dotted with forty-seven felony arrests ranging from forgery to burglary to arson.

Berry went to interview Cox, who was at Pendleton. "When Parker talked to you while you were working next to each other," he asked, "he told you that he wanted to use this story as a lever, right?"

"Yes."

"What did he say?"

"He said his girl friend had the wreck, that she hit the guy trotting down the side of the road, and he was worried about how much trouble she would be in if he went ahead with his story. He said his girl friend had done it and that he was willing to testify to that fact if it would help him. He asked my advice."

Berry was fascinated. "What did you tell him?"

"I told him he had a hell of a mess," answered Cox, sucking deeply on his cigarette.

In sworn testimony later, Kim Randle told Berry that she was either at work or at home on the night of March 16, not in Bloomington, and that she was willing to submit to a polygraph test and to hypnosis to verify her statement.

Berry's eyes flashed. "Did Reggie Parker ever tell you why he fabricated this story and gave it to David Colman?'' he asked.

"To test him or whatever," she said. "I don't completely understand it. He was in a manic-depressive state at the time. That's my opinion. It upset me . . . what he said and all, but he was thinking that everybody had given up on him. Being alone, just being away from society and all, you think all kinds of crazy thoughts. In places like that you don't have many friends. They're not good people in places like that.''

Berry was baffled. The Reggie Parker escapade, this hoax, had accomplished nothing more than to take him around in a series of maddening circles. What's more, he was no closer to identifying positively the driver of the car that hit Heidenreich than he was when this crazy charade began. Obviously, he would have a lot more work to do before the mystery was solved.

14

Before 1972, the Olympic Games were a spectacle that appeared in the newspapers every four years, but as long as the United States did well the American public's collective ego was sufficiently massaged and not much thought was given to the Games for four more years. After they were over, Americans turned their attention to the stretch drives of major league baseball and the start of the football season and the names of athletes that they recognized. Most of the Olympians faded into the background and continued to train in anonymity, resigned to the fact that this was the way the system worked. Their rewards were mostly of the spirit.

Television changed all this at Munich in 1972. The Olympic Games were beamed daily into the living rooms of America and for two weeks Americans sat fascinated as they watched swimmer Mark Spitz, gymnast Olga Korbut of Russia and Frank Shorter, the first American to win a gold medal in the marathon in sixty-four years. The threats to American supremacy by the Soviet Union and by East Germany in a number of sports and the seemingly endless series of reversals that tormented American athletes—especially where borderline decisions by iron-curtain judges appeared questionable—heightened American awareness.

The bitterest of the U.S. defeats was in basketball when a

184

chaotic finish in which the Soviet Union was allowed to put the ball into play three times resulted in a 51–50 Russian victory and a protest by the U.S. that was rejected by an uncompromising Olympic jury.

The Russian win touched off patriotic anger in America that quickly intensified a crusade to place more importance on the Olympic movement. The large number of medals being won by the communist-bloc countries embarrassed Americans.

The true sportsman will say he abhors the emphasis on the medal count, that it completely counters the philosophy of the founder of the modern Olympic Games, French nobleman Pierre de Coubertin, who wrote: "The important thing in the Olympic Games is not winning, but in taking part." However, the iron-curtain countries have shrewdly equated the medal totals with the importance and proficiency of their socialistic systems.

Shorter's victory in the marathon at Munich was the catalyst for the upsurge of running and jogging in America. At Montreal in 1976 the television cameras again followed the marathoners through the city streets and parks as they had four years earlier in Munich. This type of race was naturally more compelling for the American viewer than a track meet where the scenery never changed.

The Games at Moscow in 1980 will be the first held behind the Iron Curtain. The Soviet Union hopes to use this opportunity for a propaganda blitz to show the world that it can conduct an Olympics without the political intransigence that blemished Munich and Montreal. The 1980 Games will become a television spectacle unequaled by any previous media event, sports or otherwise. NBC, which paid $85 million for the rights—in negotiations conducted by German impresario Lothar Bock and shrouded in intrigue—will televise 150 hours during the two weeks of the Games, which is double the amount of coverage we had from Montreal.

"There is greater emphasis on amateur sports now than at any other time in history across the world and television of the Olympics helped greatly to engender this interest," says Robert Kane, president of the United States Olympic Committee. "One billion people watched the Olympics from Montreal. Amateur sports have opened up nations to each other. Although the Iron Curtain has been drawn for a long time, the Soviet Union is now making a deliberate effort. When a country is a host to the Olympics it invites the entire world.''

There is no question that before the current Olympiad, the four-year period between Montreal and Moscow, the fragmented nature of amateur sports in the U.S. prevented this nation from always sending its best teams to the Games, and from creating a central policymaking body to establish direction and to raise money. Many sports under the aegis of the USOC or the Amateur Athletic Union have been unable effectively to develop athletes because of a lack of funds.

The endemic feuds and jurisdictional disputes that erupted between the fractious bodies, the Amateur Athletic Union (AAU) and the National Collegiate Athletic Association (NCAA), the controlling body of the nation's colleges, have for decades prevented America's Olympic movement from proceeding with any sense of order. That American athletes were successful in international competition was more a result of their own tireless pursuits and pride than because of national objectives. The athletes have been at the mercy of any number of controlling bodies in America, all trying to establish and retain a power base within the system. While these bodies squabbled among themselves, other countries began to surpass America because their superior organized systems were better preparing their athletes.

But finally some changes are being effected. After half a century of an Olympic program that has done practically nothing more than spin its wheels because of infighting and because of the USOC's insistence that it had no funds, Congress in 1978 voted into law the Amateur Sports Act and gave $16 million to the USOC. Until then, the U.S. was the only country in the membership of the International Olympic Committee that received no financial support from its federal government.

The Amateur Sports Act is an outgrowth of the President's Commission on Olympic Sports, a body that was empowered during President Gerald Ford's term. The commission spent $1 million and eighteen months analyzing and restructuring much of the entire U.S. amateur sports system. The commission was dissolved when Ford left office but most of its recommendations were absorbed into the Amateur Sports Act.

The reform voted by Congress establishes the USOC as the influential and coordinating body of amateur athletics in the U.S. It does not, however, eliminate the political dissension or jealousies between the AAU and the NCAA. Traditionally, the AAU was the controlling body of amateur athletics, but the NCAA is now the more powerful of the two. The USOC will serve as a forum for an athlete or a sport to turn to if there is a grievance. If the dispute cannot be settled, the next step will be the American Arbitration Association. Despite partisan outcries, the Amateur Sports Act will lead to beneficial change. It provides for the national governing body of each Olympic sport in America to become an autonomous working member of the USOC by 1980, thus strengthening the national effort in building effective Olympic teams. Both the NCAA and AAU will be represented on the national governing bodies. This dual representation will do something to curb the political jealousy and divisiveness of the two organizations—factors that have continally threatened the rights of American athletes to free competition and access to training facilities.

In 1972 Vince Matthews had to climb three fences daily to train at a high school track in Brooklyn. He then had to raise money to pay his way to the Olympic Trials. At Munich, he won the gold medal in the 400. "The public becomes outraged," says Robert Helmick, president of the AAU, "when Olympians are affected by facilities being closed to them—when they have to scrounge, beg or sneak into swimming pools or athletic fields to train. I'm outraged that our youth, not just our Olympians, can't take full advantage of facilities."

American athletes would like to be able to concentrate on sports rather than politics. But the horror stories they tell of being blocked at every turn by the AAU and NCAA are documented and have proliferated through the years. The Amateur Sports Act includes an Athlete Bill of Rights, but the delicate compromising negotiations between the AAU and NCAA have diluted it.

The athletes have been trapped in the crossfire between the two bodies, both of which have attempted to protect their fiefdoms by tightly controlling the national governing bodies under their umbrellas. The NCAA maintains it must direct athletes at its member schools, that to permit an athlete to choose between a school's scheduled event and participation in one elsewhere would lead to chaos.

The quarrelling between the AAU and NCAA has been most vocal over jurisdiction of four sports—track and field, basketball, gymnastics, and wrestling. Both bodies have sponsored programs in these sports and when the question of international accreditation arose regarding American athletes, both bodies have assumed a cavalier attitude toward each other. The NCAA withheld basketball players from international competition in opposition to the AAU, and then left the USOC, claiming the AAU controlled it. It since has been reseated as a USOC member.

The needs of the American Olympic movement have clearly been identified and met in the Amateur Sports Act. The effects will be more recognizable in the performances by Americans in the 1984 Olympics at Los Angeles than in 1980 at Moscow: Decades of mistakes and disorganization cannot be made up immediately. Still, for the first time in America the national governing bodies are working toward a single objective—amateur programs designed for amateur athletes and Olympic teams that will be properly prepared.

"Until now," says Frank Shorter, "absolutely nothing has been done for the American athlete. All I ask is to be able to step to the line for an Olympic final, to look to the left and to the right, and not feel that I'm standing there, an American, at a disadvantage." He speaks of athletes in countries who are financed while they train, either by the government or by clubs bankrolled by industry or the government, of lavishly equipped training centers, of national sports medicine programs that keep the athlete a finely tuned machine. IOC rules limit government influence in Olympic sports and define what amateurism is. However, the Soviet Union and East Germany interpret the mandates on amateurism differently than does the U.S. and are said to subsidize their very best athletes at a level that would be considered professional in the U.S.

"The U.S. concept of amateurism is hypocrisy," says Olympian Craig Virgin, one of America's rising young distance aces. "This country is going to have to quit shutting its eyes to what is going on. If the AAU or the USOC wants to control the track and field athletes who are trying to attain financial security through road racing or through sports equipment companies or by competing in meets in Europe, something in the U.S. is going to have to be offered that is just as good and is legally acceptable so the athlete does not have to hide his earnings. The individual athlete who is willing to hustle his own deals, either with a shoe company or a backer or meet promoters, has the best chance right now.

"As an American I've been used to a free system, independence, and control over my destiny. You won't find many Americans who would be willing to put up with the computerized training systems that the Russians and the East Germans are working with. Americans have been too independent and too human for too long to feel comfortable in a situation like that."

Garry Bjorklund, also an Olympian, is from the tiny town of Twig, Minnesota. He lives in Minneapolis where he trains and owns Garry Bjorklund Sports, a business outlet that evolved from his athletic shoe business, Body and Sole. He ran at the University of Minnesota where he won three successive Big Ten Conference cross-country championships. "I wanted to continue running after college but I needed financial help," says Bjorklund. "I used traditional methods in soliciting assistance from the community. I went to an organization and said, 'Hey, I'm Garry Bjorklund and I'm training for the Olympics. Will you help me?' The attitude I got was, 'Get lost, kid!' But once you make the team you become very significant in the community. They are suddenly proud of you and their services are available to you. We don't even have a good grass-roots program in America. In Minneapolis, there is not much being done for the kids except a few token age-group meets. Part of it is the fault of our athletes in the U.S. They don't try to communicate the message of sports to the kids. There are a lot of problems, but the biggest is that the whole system has perpetuated itself."

Money—lots of it—could alleviate much of the dilemma that has stalked the Olympic movement in America for years. The USOC has doubled its budget from $13 million to $26 million for the quadrennium of 1976 to 1980. Of this total, $9.3 million is going to thirty-three national governing bodies. From 1972 to 1976, the thirty-three bodies had $2.2 million to work with. "More has been done in the last year and a half than in the previous fifty years," Kane, asserts. "When the American public thinks of the Olympic Games it is not thinking about all the sports, it's thinking of the three or four that get all the publicity. In the past the USOC pretty much followed the mandate of Public Law 805 (under which it is chartered), which was to choose an Olympic team and raise money to send it. Now we're making sure some of the less developed sports receive money because they they don't have the means themselves of raising it. It puts the onus on them to do the best they can with this money. While the money may not be in the totals they'd like, it is still more than they have had ever before. Private corporations have contributed to us in the past but never as generously as now. This is certainly the high point in Olympic support in this country."

Jimmy Carnes, formerly the head track and field coach at the University of Florida, is chairman of the AAU Track and Field Committee and he will be the head coach of the American men's team at Moscow. When he took office in 1977 his Track and Field Committee owed the AAU general fund $150,000. One year later the debt was paid off. "We could solve the whole financial thing immediately if all the people who are associated with track and field or running in America would pay the $3.50 AAU membership fee," says Carnes. "We'd then have enough money to hire a staff of people we need to produce the best Olympic team we can. We already have the best development system in the world with our high schools and colleges. If all the track coaches in America volunteered to help us, to go to the private sector and raise big dollars, we could generate the enthusiasm we need to get the job done."

The athletes are speaking up, too. "Their opinions now are respected while their actions and their performances are being watched by millions of people," says Stan Vinson, one of the world's leading 400-meter runners. "The athletes are saying, 'America needs to do more for its own,' and maybe the people will listen. If the American people want to win on an international level, and they have shown that they do, then they should do something for those who are going out to do the competing for them."

Decades of inadequate funding, and indifference to the training of America's Olympians, have led to bad feelings among the athletes. A few have claimed that the medals they won were a credit to their own efforts and that their country should not share in the achievement.

Arnie Robinson, gold medalist at Montreal in the long jump, says, "When I was on the victory stand and listening to the National Anthem, it was a satisfying and proud moment. Yet, realistically, this country should do a lot better for its amateur athletes and has no right to take credit for their accomplishments or to say that the athlete's medals are the country's medals. I will bet that fewer than ten percent of our Olympians are thinking 'country' when they compete or are motivated by some old-fashioned concept of competing for the red, white, and blue."

The object of the athletes' discomfiture has been the AAU ("the string that makes the monkey dance," as Bjorklund describes it). The athletes claim that although the AAU controls much of their actions the AAU pronouncements of intended care for the athletes' welfare are transparent.

The AAU handbook outlines procedure for international travel by American athletes, for example, for reimbursement of per diem, and it defines an amateur. "It is a one-sided contract," says Bjorklund. "The minute you become an AAU athlete you literally become an indentured servant. They hold all power over you. An athlete cannot compete anywhere in the world without the sanction of the AAU and those conditions oftentimes are ludicrous.

"We in America will always be competitive because there are enough parents like mine who will say, 'Look, if it's important enough to you we will bankroll you.'

"It seems to me that neither the AAU nor the IAAF [International Amateur Athletic Federation, the governing body of all amateur sports] is there to promote sports; only to control the athlete and the revenues derived from sports. In controlling the athlete they make him completely dependent upon them. We don't need that in America."

Heavy criticism. Yet Jimmy Carnes defends the AAU just as strenuously, arguing that it is a misunderstood organization and that most of the medals won by the U.S. through the years can be credited to the AAU.

The contentiousness and the political backbiting of amateur sports in America have served to widen the schism of uneasy feelings between the athlete and those in control, some of whom have been hidebound bureaucrats. Marathoner Kenny Moore, who finished fourteenth at Mexico City in 1968 and fourth at Munich in 1972, has had more than a cursory look at the infighting. Track and field has not been the only victim of it. "When tennis was an amateur sport," says Moore, "Billie Jean King woke up one day to the wrongs. She said, 'We realized that the tennis officials had no reason for being there except to disqualify people; to hunt around for reasons why people could not compete. The amateur regulations were such that this was the only power the officials had and, therefore, within the rules, the job they felt they had was to ruin people.'

"There is a fundamental difference between the way the athletes and amateur officialdom feel about the particular sport. To the athletes competing, the sport is the most important thing in the world. Officialdom feels that it can't have a role in the system unless it is keeping the athlete from a means to the end. An athlete hunting for anything to further his reason, which is to compete, is not going to worry where the money he needs comes from."

Moore was a member of the President's Commission on Olympic Sports, which found that American performances have deteriorated against athletes from countries which place a far greater emphasis on Olympic medals. Essentially, it is because of poor organization in America, where there has never been a binding system of coordination. "There are three basic modes of sports organizations employed by successful sporting nations," the commission found. "In one, government is in control. In another, a non-government sports authority is in control. In the third, no one is in control. Only the U.S. uses the third method." Through 1968, officials and coaches in this country were, with a few exceptions, synonomous. "There were AAU people and coaches who were authoritarian and wanted the athletes to stay in their places," says Moore. "Since then it is notable that the coaches have taken the side of the athletes."

George Woods, now a college admissions counselor, remains a skeptic, because of unfortunate experiences he had at Mexico City and Munich. He was the silver medalist in the shot-put at both Games but might have been the winner of golds. At Mexico City he competed with an injured wrist but the USOC medical staff neglected to tell him that he could have put protective taping on the wrist. Woods learned this was possible when he was on the field for the preliminary throws. Three shot-putters from other countries had their wrists taped and were carrying with them necessary medical certificates. Woods had only one good throw in the final round because of his pain but it was enough to squeeze out second place. "I was terribly frustrated," says Woods. "I asked the U.S. doctors if I could have worn tape and they said they would check. Hours later they came to me and told me I could have. Why hadn't someone told me before? I let them know exactly how I felt."

At Munich, Woods was ready with his medical certificate when the shot-putters walked onto the field for their preliminary throws. Adrian Paulen of The Netherlands, a member of the IOC Technical Committee then, demanded to see Woods' certificate. It was Paulen who had been in the midst of a controversy earlier in which poles used by U.S. pole vaulters at Munich were banned.

"Paulen said, 'Where's the certificate?'" recalls Woods. "I immediately thought of the vault mess and said to myself, 'Here it goes again.' I rolled my eyes and said, 'Aw, shit.' "

After a heated exchange about the use of the obscenity, Paulen went into the stands to confer with IOC members in attendance, urging the ouster of Woods. U.S. officials later soothed the ruffled feelings.

The next day, Woods had one throw left in the final round at Munich and he trailed leader Wladyslaw Komar of Poland by a centimeter, one-half an inch. Woods's heave landed in the area of the thin metal rod marking Komar's best throw. The marker was bent flat. There was confusion as the officials measured. Woods said to an official: "What's the story? If there's a question, give me another throw." An official replied: "No . . . no. We've made up our minds that your throw hit the ground first and bounced into the marker." Woods accepted the ruling.

"They took the three medal winners into a room, wiped the sweat off our faces, actually powdered our noses and we went out for the medal ceremony," says Woods. "It was later that I was told that videotapes showed that my final throw appeared to have hit the marker on the fly, which means that my throw had to have been farther than Komar's. But a protest has to be registered within twenty minutes of the end of the event and at that time I was still getting my nose powdered. I didn't know what had happened.

"When I returned to the Olympic Village one of the U.S. managers said to me, 'George, I was so disappointed for you. I saw your shot hit the stake.' I said, 'Thank you.' Does anyone think a Russian official would have done that? He would have been on that field in a minute, screaming bloody murder. Our team official sits in the stands and feels sorry for me and doesn't leave his seat to protest. Well, that just doesn't get it done. The Olympics revolve around the IOC and not the athlete. The athletes, to the IOC, are just mud on the feet to be wiped off and discarded. I grew up thinking of the Olympics as the ideal and that the man who trains hard and makes the sacrifices will win. I learned otherwise."

In 1968 the German Democratic Republic burst onto the scene at the Games in Mexico City and continued its startling rise in

1972 at Munich as such a dominant force that there were rumors the East Germans were operating a factory that mass-produced Olympic athletes. In 1976 the GDR invited a small group of journalists to visit the nation and investigate for themselves within imposed limits how, in such a short time, a small country could make this impact on the Olympic Games, historically not its province, and reap a harvest of Olympic medals.

What the journalists found was an emphasis on the training of coaches and an intricate sports medicine program that has as its goal five hundred specialists to work with athletes by 1980. The salutory effects are possible because of organization; a socialist state can organize its system any way it pleases.

East Germany is spending what is thought to be $100 million a year on its sports program. Young students are graded in different sports and then moved to a school specializing in the sport of a particular student's proficiency. In the College of Physical Culture at Leipzig the government subsidizes the students. The school has a reported budget of $8 million, which is a gift from the state and is provided by taxing industry profits. Competition is furnished by sports clubs across the country and by the Spartakiad, an intensive program for youths.

The GDR's elite athletes are monitored daily by coaches and computers, which can quickly give printouts with up-to-the-minute information on cardiovascular status, lactic acid levels in the blood, or any other important data.

The American athlete wants to see some of the East German enthusiasm implemented in the U.S. but not at the expense of his freedoms. "We're not East Germany," says Garry Bjorklund. "We're a very large and very diverse country. In theory, the things the East European countries project have merit but in the U.S. they are impractical. A more realistic approach here would be to test our athletes as was done in 1975 at the Aerobics Center in Dallas. Two things this country could provide its Olympic athletes are quality competition and accurate information. Give me a chance to compare myself statistically against other athletes in the world. Let me have a muscle biopsy and a stress test three times a year. Let me have my diet and my blood analyzed and tell me when I'm overworking or underworking. Most athletes in this country who make it to the Olympics have had to research their sport so thoroughly they have become professionals, if you will. Often, the athletes are many times more competent because of their self-acquired knowledge than some of the coaches and other officials."

The demands of the American Olympian are straightforward: an end to the pontificating by some amateur officials in high places; training centers where the athletes can go to be processed both psychologically and physiologically; a sophisticated sports medicine program that can keep him as fit as any athlete in the world; more quality competition; and funds to keep the Olympic movement strong enough so he does not feel he is training in vain while athletes in other countries are making bigger strides because of superior advantages.

Sam Bell is chairman of the AAU Track and Field Development Committee. His committee is listening to what the athletes are saying. Augmenting Bell's committee is the newly formed Track and Field Association of the United States of America. Another area of improvement was suggested by Dr. Chet Jastremski, one of the five USOC staff physicians at Montreal and a member of the medical commission of the International Swimming Federation. "In the East European countries," says Dr. Jastremski, "sports medicine helps decide what sport the athlete will be best suited for by measuring leg length, body size, everything. In the U.S. we don't have to do that. We have a large population and people participating at all levels and so we have a natural selection of athletes.

"What we don't have are national publications that can disseminate information on each sport; this is where we need our education. Many journals are theoretical and not practical. There are children under twelve, who haven't reached their growth potential, doing weight training and risking damage to joints because coaches don't know of the dangers. Each sport should have its own full-time medical staff that would enable doctors to go to where the athlete is in training. To take an athlete out of his environment, interrupt his cycle of workouts and ask him to go somewhere else for a few days could be detrimental to his development.

"Nor can we ethically provide testing for only our best athletes. Who is to say that one American is better than another? They may make that distinction in East Germany. But if I'm going to provide a blood test for the pole vaulter who has gone 17–9, should I not provide one for the vaulter who has gone 17–6? We have many vaulters in the latter category."

Consider the gap between rhetoric and reality. The restrictive nature of the IOC and IAAF definitions of amateurism has fostered hypocrisy and has erected a lot of very handy straw men. That under-the-table payments are made to amateur athletes is a conveniently ignored secret. The athletes conceal the payments from the AAU and international officials for fear of reprisal. For some American Olympians, payoffs are a major means of support. A top name can earn $1,000 a meet with bonuses for outstanding performances in Europe. The indoor circuit in the U.S. can be lucrative for top athletes and road runs are becoming so. A shoe company will pay an athlete as much as $30,000 a year to wear its product. Other forms of payoff include extra per diem, merchandise, and air fare differential. Athletes given first-class round-trip tickets by promoters can exchange them for tourist accomodations and pocket the difference. It's all illegal, of course. The AAU travel permit, a necessary item for any athlete wishing to compete abroad, states: "Our permission is given with the understanding that the athlete concerned will not ask for nor accept reimbursement for any expenses in connection with his travel to and from the countries. The competition in which the athlete participates must submit to this [AAU] office a copy of any consideration that might be advanced."

The President's Commission on Olympic Sports acknowledged the chagrin of U.S. amateurs having to compete against state-subsidized professionals. The commission concluded, "The IOC, preferring to keep the Olympic movement unified rather than uniform, will not suspend state-supported athletes." But the commission, recognizing the plight of American Olympians, recommended a liberalization of U.S. standards where they are stricter than is required by international bodies and stated, as a matter of policy, that athletes should be able to accept revenues such as endorsements in advertising and honorariums for public appearances or speeches.

The Olympic Games are certainly flawed, making, as they do, the distinction between an athlete who is a hypocrite—the amateur who accepts payment—and the prohibited professional, who is an acceptable "amateur." The IOC is an autocratic body that chooses its own successors and seemingly cannot come to grips with the demand by the Western world that the Games be open to all. The IOC's Games, as they are now, would surely die without approval of changes by the communist nations, and they are happy with things as they are.

At Munich in 1972, George Woods sat in on a conversation between America's Jay Silvester and Sweden's Ricky Bruch after Silvester had finished second and Bruch third in the discus throw. "Bruch was shaking his head sadly," recalls Woods. "Jay asked him what was wrong. Bruch said, 'If I had won the gold medal I had been promised $120,000 in endorsements. As it is, I won the bronze and that's worth only $30,000.' Jay is sitting there thinking, 'Gee, when I get back home to Utah I'll get zero. Absolutely nothing.' So where's it at?"

Before Munich and the increased television exposure, few American track and field athletes could say they capitalized on their Olympic fame. Since Munich, that is no longer true even though professional track, the International Track Association, flopped because of small crowds at its meets in the U.S., most of them indoor, and the even smaller TV ratings. But at that, the number of athletes profiting is miniscule. Three of them, Frank Shorter, Marty Liquori and Garry Bjorklund, are in business with sporting goods outlets. Bruce Jenner became the Montreal Games' most marketable hero after he won the gold medal in the decathlon.

Imperfect though they are, the Olympic Games offer the joy of competition that transcends the ambiguities of the Games. Hayes Jones is today an executive with American Airlines Inc. In 1964, high hurdler Jones won the gold medal at Tokyo, providing him with striking memories of the Olympics, of the courage and the disappointment and the beauty of it all.

In 1962, while preparing for the Games at Tokyo, Jones got married. The athletic director at his school told him he had just traded a gold medal for a bride. "I began to lose," says Jones, remembering the words of the athletic director. "I wanted to quit, and I would have but my wife Odeene would not let me. But when I got to Tokyo I knew my training had not been right, that I had not done enough speed work. I was slow between the hurdles.

"On the day of the finals I ran up and down in the tunnel under the stadium, trying somehow at the last minute to find speed. My wife was in the stands with Jesse Owens. She began to cry. She was convinced I was going to lose. In the tunnel a coaching friend, Ed Temple, came to me and said, 'Listen, Hayes, forget about your speed. Just run between the hurdles. Just run.' "

There were five bunched together as the tape snapped: Jones, Blaine Lindgren of the U.S., Anatoly Mikhailov, a Russian, Eddy Ottoz of Italy and Gurbachan Randhawa of India. "At first I thought the Russian had won because his coach came out and hugged him," says Jones. "An Indian coach was congratulating his runner. My coach was standing there with a cigarette in his mouth. It seemed forever before the lights came on the scoreboard. Then it came: 'J . . . O . . . N . . . E . . . S . . .'

"I can't tell you the feeling, the thrill of it."

Jones gave his gold medal to the children of Pontiac, Michigan, his home town. The medal is on display there today at the Pontiac Municipal Building.

"It wasn't the medal that mattered, don't you see?" says Jones softly. "It was the experience. When I think of the Olympic Games today I don't think of the medal. I think of my wife and Jesse Owens; my wife crying and me in that tunnel trying to get something I did not have and I think of that scoreboard lighting up:
'J . . . O . . . N . . . E . . . S . . .' "

For Garry Bjorklund, the Olympics are an embodiment of a driving vision. He labored for ninety cents an hour as a bus boy at a Baton Rouge, Louisiana, restaurant in 1974 while in training for the 1976 Games. He was invited to help coach the distance runners at Louisiana State University. "It was a bust," he says. "The job title was no more than a ham sandwich. But in four months of working in the restaurant I saved enough money to buy an old car. I went to the only other place in the United States I thought I could go." That was Boulder, Colorado, where a friend let him stay at his home free. There, he worked as a janitor and trained until he was ready.

Triple jumper James Butts placed second at Montreal, the first American to win a medal in his event since 1928. That he held himself together emotionally through the Games was an accomplishment in itself. He had supported himself, his mother, and his sister by working at two jobs. He trained from five to seven each morning. Fifty minutes later he was on duty as a security guard at a department store in Los Angeles. His shift was over at 4:50. At 7:00 P.M. he clocked in at the UCLA Medical Center where he worked until 11:00 delivering laundry.

The solutions for reform of the antiquated and unrealistic U.S. Olympic system offered by official and athlete alike revolve around a stipend. Some favor it, some oppose it. Frank Shorter, Garry Bjorklund and Jimmy Carnes caution against its use. Shorter and Bjorklund say that American athletes do not want handouts, equating stipends to welfare, but want an opportunity to earn their own way. "I'm not in favor of subsidizing an athlete to live so he can train," says Carnes. "I am in favor of development and helping him get competition and providing him with facilities to train. If a man is married he should not have to take his food money to get to the competition he needs. We should take care of that. I say if we do that, the athlete can survive very well in America. The athletes who say, 'You've never done anything for me' are being unfair. The AAU may have paid his way to Russia or elsewhere, fed him, housed him, given him a uniform and the competition which enabled him to be a better athlete."

Two other items that rank high on the athletes' list of needs —training centers and a sports medicine program—are becoming realities. Some of the $16 million voted by Congress in

1978 will be used by the USOC to enlarge the sports medicine program, concentrating on bio-mechanics, nutrition, physiology, sports psychology, and injury rehabilitation. Money will be available for testing such as that done at the Aerobics Center in Dallas in 1975. Some of the $16 million will be used for permanent training centers that have been established at Colorado Springs, Colorado, also the headquarters of the USOC, and at Squaw Valley, California. The third center will be at Lake Placid, New York, the site of the 1980 Winter Olympic Games. "These centers are available to the Olympic national governing bodies on an elective basis," says Jerry Lace, director of operations for the USOC. "We are providing them but we're not saying they have to come and use them. We envision five hundred athletes a day during the summer months using the centers, with different teams moving in and out. If we don't have the room for everyone we can set up auxiliary centers at colleges across the country when they are not in session. We don't tell the governing bodies how to run their programs. Sports medicine, directing the centers, hotel services, and transportation is our thing. The USOC will not try to beef up one sport because it offers the best possibility of a sweep of all the medals at the next Olympics. The East Germans do that. We want to be consistent and offer the same opportunities to all our sports, saying only, 'If you want to be the best, here are the things required to reach that level.' "

James Butts and Stan Vinson want the emphasis on training centers. "The athletes keep waiting for some help," says Butts. "That's why I keep my nose clean. I was the first American to win a medal in my event in forty-eight years. That in itself should be enough for them to know that I have a gift and hopefully they'd say, 'Hey, let's don't let him die. Let's keep him motivated so he can excel.' All that I want is a place where I can work out in an atmosphere of fresh air and good food."

And a staff of doctors and coaches, adds Vinson. "The athlete needs to be monitored," he says. "I've been training constantly since 1969. That's incredible when one thinks of the vacations I've given up and the sacrifices I've made. But an athlete knows what he must do to stay on top: He has to hurt sometimes and he has to work."

Shouldering the developmental program, Sam Bell is starting from the ground floor by placing the challenges in the hands of the coaches, as the East Germans are doing. "What we've got to do is to be sure we develop as much technical knowledge throughout the whole country; try to take the knowledge to the communities," says Bell. "We have to enhance technical skills and get more information disseminated and we're doing that in the developmental learn-by-doing clinics. There, our coaches, through step-by-step teaching progressions, learn thoroughly the events they will be instructing. The East Europeans test their coaches before elevating them to different levels. There might be merit in America following some form of that."

For years the U.S. sent its athletes and coaches abroad as goodwill ambassadors and they passed along information, on techniques in events, that has quickened the development of other countries. Now, all nations borrow from each other. "We had the first seven-foot high-jumper, Charley Dumas," says Bell, "and we dominated the event until 1960 when the Russians won the gold medal. What happened is that they showed us the value of speed in the approach to the jump. In 1968, after Dick Fosbury won the high jump with the 'Fosbury Flop' at Mexico City, the Russian coach said to me, 'It's criminal that someone would win with that kind of technique.' But they began to use it. Poland has learned the vault from us while we have learned a lot about the triple jump from the Russians and the Poles."

Bell wants America to follow the practice of many other countries and select a national track and field team. "It can be three or four people per event," explains Bell. "Once we pick it we must do some things for the athletes. Provide them with funds to get to meets, and funds to go somewhere to be coached if they aren't getting coaching where they live. Provide them with a film library of themselves and of others in the world and give them technical data on what others are doing. Once we pick that team we've got to spend $8,000 a year on our very best athletes, who can be selected by performance and potential. There are things

I'd require from them in return. We have to get to that point where we say to the athletes: 'You have to do more than just represent your country every four years at the Olympics.'

"I foresee us providing that athlete on the national team a stipend of maybe $300 a month. It would give him the freedom to train and still supplement the stipend with some other means, and he won't have to work eight hours a day to stay alive so he can train. It could change the whole attitude of those athletes who have no loyalty to the country. They would know they aren't having to do it all by themselves. Then, if we name a national coach, we need to build a list of twenty-five coaches under him in each event who are capable of proper instruction in all parts of the nation."

Bell would not change the method of selecting the U.S. Olympic track and field team. "Head-to-head competition is the best way at the Trials, regardless of all previous performances," he says.

Americans are not characterized by great patience. They want results but they want them quickly so they can move on to something else. Americans want to be the best in international competition, but when they have been asked to pay the cost of being the best they have stepped back, insisting instead that the amateur athlete should reach his goal on his own because it is the American way. The work ethic.

The concerned corporate community may be the savior of the Olympic movement in America. Many of the sports are now sponsored by dollars from the private sector.

It was the combination of circumstances and the specter of the powerful teams from the Soviet Union and East Germany that started Howard Miller, president of the Canteen Corporation, thinking at the Games in Montreal. He watched the awesome precision of the swimmers, gymnasts, runners, jumpers, boxers, canoeists, cyclists, and weightlifters from East European nations. After the joyful closing ceremonies, Miller began to wonder if the U.S. athletes would be embarrassed in 1980. Four years was barely enough time to prepare for Moscow, perhaps the mightiest challenge yet for America's Olympians.

Miller proposed to the USOC a Job Opportunity Program in which an athlete is hired by a firm and receives a salary but is given paid time off to train. The USOC approved the idea and the program was an instant success. Applicants exceeded the available jobs. Because of the huge number of requests, the USOC was forced to recommend for jobs only those athletes who have a chance to make the 1980 Olympic team. If an athlete who is hired fails to make the 1980 team his status becomes that of any other employee and he can be retained or released by the firm. The Canteen Corporation and Hal Berge, administrator of the program, do not select the athletes. The names are provided by the USOC to Canteen, which places the athletes with an ever-growing number of corporations that are participating in the program.

Among those employed by Canteen are Tom Burleson and 1976 gold medalist speed skater Peter Mueller, a maître d' at a Milwaukee restaurant. Mueller's wife, Leah Paulos, 1976 silver medalist speed skater, is a sales representative in the program. Canteen located a position for Stan Vinson as a customer service representative at Wilson Sporting Goods in Chicago.

Steve Heidenreich was hired as a sales trainee by Cook Incorporated, a Bloomington firm that manufactures surgical products. Although he did not obtain the position through the Job Opportunity Program, it was tailored exactly like those jobs. He was able to leave the office early each afternoon to train, and this, of course, was an ideal situation for him. The new job gave his life cohesion and reconciled his problem with division of his precious time.

The USOC wheel is moving in a widening circle. In addition to the Job Opportunity Program, a Broken-Time Program has been put into effect in which an athlete is reimbursed for a loss of wages while he trains and competes.

Slowly, the USOC is making up lost ground. The price tag will be enormous if America wants to compete on an equal basis with the state-subsidized athletes. But the USOC is examining ways to improve the esoteric sports that have been weak.

"Identification and selection is the answer," says Jerry Lace. "I envision some day high school athletes being asked, 'I know you play basketball now but how would you like to go to the Olympic Games? I'm not guaranteeing you a spot but here's a sport where we need help.' It may be luge or archery or whatever. We do not have as many luge or bobsled runs in this country as we have gymnasiums and swimming pools. Consequently, the less popular sports have suffered. We need the good athlete. This is how East Germany approaches it—but without the freedom of selection of a sport by the athlete."

The real hope and glory of the Olympic Games remains fixed in the individual Olympian and his ability to ignore the politics, the foibles, the faults that obscure the competition and the splendor. If the individual can do this then the Games have a chance. What is an Olympian? It is implacable Garry Bjorklund running the last mile and a half of the 10,000 at the 1976 Trials in Eugene, Oregon, without his left shoe—that had come off when a runner behind him stepped on his foot.

The crowd, captured by his courage, began a thunderous chant:

". . . Bee-Jay!

". . . Bee-Jay!"

His desperate kick caught Bill Rodgers and he claimed the third and last spot on the team by four yards. "I hope that's what it's like to enter the gates of heaven," says Bjorklund. "I couldn't sleep for three nights and I get knots in my stomach when I think about it now.

"The first night I lay awake, and although I'm not a vicious person, I thought about all the people who had made it difficult for me to do what I had done. I hoped they were watching on television because it didn't belong to them at all. What I want to say to America is: 'If you want an Olympian . . . be for that Olympian.' "

In the autumn of 1978, Heidenreich was running better than he ever had in his life at distances from five to eight miles, averaging times of five minutes a mile in road races. Following a hard workout one afternoon he stopped at Sam Bell's office.

"Coach," he said, wiping the perspiration from his eyes, "you know that some day I'd like to run in the Olympics. Tell me what you think I have to do to get there."

Bell paced silently for a few minutes. "I'll give it to you straight, Heidi," he said. "You are going to have to stay injury-free. You don't have a real heavy bone frame and you have a history of injuries. Keeping healthy is going to have to be such a commitment that unless everything you do revolves around it, you probably won't have a chance of becoming an Olympian.

"You're going to have to develop self-discipline about going overboard in your training. You've got to go at it one day at a time, have patience, and be willing to work hard on the days you work hard and rest on the days you rest. You have to know when to stop, and I as a coach have to recognize when to tell you to turn it on or turn it off.

"You need a broad aerobics foundation and you're getting it. But have patience, please. You're running great at longer distances now and hanging on longer in each race.

"I'm very proud of you. You've made phenomenal strides since the accident . . . just unbelievable. I don't think anyone really understands how far you have come back. When I saw you run for the first time in the fall of 1976 it almost made me weep. It was like taking a baby and teaching it to walk."

Steve smiled.

"And above all else, Heidi," continued the coach, "you must believe in yourself."

That won't be difficult. Heidi always has.

15

It was 5:30 on a Wednesday afternoon when Tom Berry turned his white Mustang into the parking lot at the law office of Don Robertson, Sonny Thorsrud's lawyer.

Berry glanced at his watch. He was not particularly eager to face the business he was about to conduct. Berry opened the main door and walked in. The office was practically deserted; the staff had left for the day. Robertson greeted him, smiling, and ushered him into a conference room.

Berry slapped his edition of the Bloomington *Herald-Telephone* on the table. He pointed to the story with the three-column headline on the front page.

NEW EVIDENCE DISCLOSED
IN HEIDENREICH INCIDENT

Bloomington Police said today that yet another link to the vehicle that may have struck former Indiana University miler Steve Heidenreich has been uncovered. A spokesman declined to elaborate. Detective Bob Sansone would neither confirm nor deny whether the new evidence was related to the "Mystery Woman" plot that last month was branded a hoax.

"Sansone called me," said Berry. "You see this?" He nodded toward the newspaper.

"Yes . . . yes, I have."

Berry looked at Robertson, his head turned slightly aside. "I always believed all that mystery woman stuff was a myth," he said. "I was convinced of it. If I hadn't been, I'd have been considerably more lenient in my settlement demands."

Robertson, known as the leading defense attorney in Bloomington, did not answer immediately, but sat quietly, gathering his thoughts. He was a soft-spoken man, the opposite of Berry. They had been classmates and friends in law school at Indiana University and they had often tangled professionally in court.

"I'm going to tell you something you don't know," Robertson said finally. "I believe I can prove that it was a van that hit Steve Heidenreich . . . with the mirror on the passenger side. And that it was not driven by Sonny Thorsrud. And I know where the van is."

Berry looked up quickly. "Oh? I'd like to see it. Tell me about it so I can check it out."

Robertson looked away. "No . . . no, I have no intention of letting you know where it is."

They were silent. For the moment, Berry let it rest. He nodded, pushed his chair back, bid Robertson goodbye and walked out into the evening.

If what Robertson said was true, Heidi could have been struck on the right side of his head as he ran north on Kinser Pike by a vehicle traveling south. Berry had considered this once before and dismissed the idea. He shook his head and climbed into his car.

The following morning Berry was in Sansone's office early. The Bloomington police were exploring all hypotheses including one, absurd as it seemed, that Heidenreich might have been trafficking in drugs and had been ordered killed by someone within the high echelon of the drug subculture.

Sansone had taken paint samples from the van and had sent them to the FBI lab in Washington, D.C. In the van's glove compartment he had found rolling papers, a syringe, and pills in plastic bags. There was also an assortment of unpaid traffic tickets.

"Tell me about vans," Berry said to Sansone. He said it casually, eager to elicit from Sansone information that he might not otherwise give him.

Sansone nodded. "Don Robertson found some guy on the west side of Indianapolis who had a van in his back yard," said Sansone.

"How?" Berry interjected.

Sansone tugged at his tie. "An anonymous letter sent to him from an inmate at the state reformatory at Pendleton," he answered. "The next thing I know is they're towing it to Bloomington. They took it to Dick Droste's Texaco station—a real mess. It had been damaged and was propped up on blocks."

"Where is the van now?"

"I don't know," said Sansone. "It disappeared."

Dick Droste happened to be one of Berry's clients. He could be a valuable contact for further information, so Berry called him.

"You remember a van that was in the station the other day?" asked Berry.

"Oh, yeah," said Droste. "The police were looking it over. This man from an auto parts place over in Greene County came and hauled it away."

"Where'd they take it—do you have any idea?"

"Lemme see. I got it. Lee's Auto Salvage. On Highway 45."

The directions were not precise. It took Berry a while before he spotted the sign—above an old wooden building leaning over so far that it looked as if it might collapse at any minute. He guided his car down a dirt driveway and stopped. He let his eyes sweep across perhaps an acre of demolished automobiles, engines, tires, and pieces of junk. "Oh God," he said.

He had started to wander through the maze of metal when suddenly a bearded man came up. He was about six feet seven inches tall, with a huge belly and a scruffy appearance.

"Whadda ya want?" he demanded.

"I'm looking for a van," answered Berry.

"Ya better see my Dad, Lee. He's in there." The man pointed to the office.

It was a ramshackle dust hole and Berry felt uncomfortable just walking into it. The tacky little room was bare except for a telephone, a wooden desk, a small adding machine, two rocking chairs with cushions, and curtains that had been crudely hung on pieces of twine. Everything was coated with oil and grease.

"I understand you're holding a van," said Berry. "I want to see it."

The man called Lee lit a long cigar. "Did Don Robertson say it was all right?"

Berry smiled. Lee had unwittingly told him what he wanted to know. The van was, indeed, on the premises.

"No, he didn't," said Berry. "Matter of fact, he doesn't know I'm here."

Lee and his son immediately moved in front of a door to a side room, blocking his passage. "You ain't gonna see it then," said Lee indignantly. He backed against the door.

Berry reached for the phone and dialed Don Robertson's number. "Don? This is Berry. I'm at Lee's Auto Salvage and Lee says I can't see the van. What do you think about that?"

Berry waited. There was no response at the other end as Robertson silently swallowed his surprise at the fact that Berry had smoked out the hiding place.

". . . Well," said Robertson at last, "I'd say that Lee's a pretty good man. I think you should respect his wishes."

With professional tact Berry outlined his plan to Robertson. "Don, we're going to do this one way or another. Are you sure you're not going to let me see it?"

"No, you can't."

Berry handed the phone to Lee. "Okay, you win," he said. "I can't see it now. But I will. I'll be back."

And he was, after filing a petition with the Lawrence Circuit Court ordering the defendant, in this case Robertson acting as Sonny Thorsrud's counsel, to make the evidence available. Judge Glenn Stieg approved the petition.

The van, it turned out, was owned by a man named LeRoy Jackson who lived in Indianapolis. Berry called him to Bloomington for a sworn deposition and learned during his questioning that he had no direct connection with either Reggie Parker, the convict, or Parker's girlfriend, Kim Randle, the "mystery woman." In his answers to some of Berry's other questions, though, Jackson was not so explicit.

"Have you talked to other persons about this van?" Berry asked him.

"A man, a Pinkerton detective agent, came out to my job and said a lawyer wanted to talk to me about it," said Jackson. "He said he thought it was involved in a hit-and-run. He wanted to buy it, so I told him okay, for seventeen hundred and ninety-five dollars, cash money, he could buy it. That's what I told him."

Berry folded his arms. "Tell me, Mr. Jackson, about the damage to this van. Tell me about the mirror on the driver's side. For instance, was it bent in any way as if an object had hit the mirror?"

"I can't say."

"The mirror on the passenger side, Mr. Jackson. Was it broken or did you ever change it?"

"I can't tell you that either now. I don't know. I really can't tell you whether the glass was broken or not. I don't recollect that I changed it."

A photo of the van that had been taken by Bloomington police then was introduced as deposition exhibit "A." Berry showed the picture to Jackson.

"This picture is of the front of the van, Mr. Jackson," said Berry. "It looks like the grill has a dent in it. Was that there when you bought it?"

"I don't know."

"You were around when these pictures were taken, weren't you?"

"No."

"You weren't? Why?"

"No. No I wasn't. I was probably sleepin'. I'd reckon that's just what I was doing. Yes sir."

Berry was becoming steadily more annoyed. "Who did you buy this van from?"

"As I recall, it was a Mr. Parker. I seen the van sitting on Eighth and Harding in Indianapolis, not quite on Harding but at the service station next door to the right, next to Harding."

"This Mr. Parker," said Berry. "Does he have a son named Reggie Parker?"

"Why yes," answered Jackson. "Why, I believe he does."

Reggie Parker and Kim Randle had already testified under oath that they were not in Bloomington on March 16, 1976. Knowing this, Berry doubted that the van was involved. LeRoy Jackson's link with Reggie Parker was through his father, and probably coincidental. Parker's father had a van to sell and LeRoy Jackson happened to buy it. Berry silently congratulated his friend, Don Robertson, for being enterprising and bold, but he sincerely believed that Robertson was chasing a clue that, instead of breaking the case, would lead him nowhere. There always was the possibility that someone else could have been driving the van. But in rereading LeRoy Jackson's deposition, Berry concluded the chances of this were remote.

Heidi was miserable at the thought of a trial and what it might bring. He had filed a $500,000 civil suit against Sonny Thorsrud, and although the trial was scheduled, it had already been postponed three times. The ballooning speculation, the swirling rumors, the innuendo of drug trafficking were anguishing. Escape from all this was very tempting. He called Tom Berry and said he wanted to talk about it. Berry advised him of what he could expect if the case went to trial.

"The media will turn this into a sensational item," said Berry. "You are well known in Indiana. So far as we know, you are the first of this country's promising young runners to have this happen—to be struck by a car and almost lose your life. That gives the story national implication and impact.

"There have been so many bizarre sidelights to this case. And neither Robertson nor I have been able to get a handle on it."

Heidenreich wanted answers, of course. However, after two years of personal suffering he was terrified at the prospect of having to relive and describe the details of the months of frustration and pain that he had experienced. The idea of discussing his rebirth before a jury seemed an unreasonable invasion of his privacy. The litigation, some of which he thought might be bitter, frightened him.

Then there was the matter of the one percent contributory clause in Indiana law that Tom Berry had warned him about. If the jury found for the defendant, there would be no monetary reward for Steve. And even if a jury ruled in favor of Heidenreich, appeals could tie up the case for years. The court would eventually make the final judgment.

Heidi took small solace in this. He was resolute . . . but he also was scared. "I want out from under all this," he said to Berry. "I want to be free."

Berry considered his request. "It's your decision, Steve. Frankly, a trial can be time-consuming, it can be expensive, it can be a strain, and it can be unpleasant. But that's only one side of it."

Heidi took two days to think about it.

"Tom," he said finally, "I want to settle out of court."

A financial figure presented to Robertson was accepted by Thorsrud's insurance company and that was that. Judge Glenn Stieg dismissed the case with prejudice, a legal term meaning that Heidenreich cannot file another suit against Sonny Thorsrud in connection with the accident. Heidi felt as if an enormous weight had been lifted from his shoulders when he walked away from the possibility of a trial.

There was the possibility that Heidi would never know positively the identification of the person who struck him down. Not unless someone stepped forward and admitted guilt, and that was unlikely. At heart he believed Sonny Thorsrud was the guilty party, but this had not been legally proved. The emergence of the van as the vehicle that might have hit him had done nothing more than deepen the intrigue, and no legal link to the accident had been established with the van, either.

What mattered most to Heidi was that his decision to settle out of court released him from the fearful pressure of a trial; and by so doing he had found something infinitely more satisfying—an inner peace he had not felt for months.

He was thoroughly wrapped up in his job at Cook Incorporated, so much that he could not wait to get to the office in the morning. He began taking work home with him at night. His scarred confidence soared. He welcomed the exactness of individual responsibility and he worked hard at it. He had made a pact with himself when he began running again that he would deny himself the sports car he had always coveted until he ran a four-minute mile. That was to be the definitive measure of his comeback, to be competitive again with any runner in the world. He soon realized that he had set his goal too high, that to run that fast again would require more time than he had realistically allotted. And besides, he said to himself, he really had earned the car, hadn't he? Hadn't he done something equal to any four-minute mile by just being alive? And his running fulfilled his need. If he had never tried to run again, how would he ever have known that he could?

He bought the car.

Not long after, as a practical investment, he purchased a house in Bloomington. His future had a long-lasting feeling to it. These were glorious days. And he was considering asking someone else to live with him in that house.

Steve's courtship of Connie was proceeding rapidly; he had become incorrigibly romantic, and each day he felt more sure that their commitment to one another was solid and real. Their relationship was developing naturally, he told Sam Bell one day as they talked. "We have a sense of freedom as a couple, not a dependency on each other like some people have. We just like to be together. One of the greatest things we have going for us is that I love Connie for what she is and she feels the same about me. There is no need for us to play roles. Our love is the ability to allow us to be what we choose, without insistence from the other that we must satisfy each other. This is possible because I love myself and Connie loves herself."

He went to Cincinnati for a week on business. The first night he was away, he sat down in his motel room, listening to the rain outside, and he wrote:

Connie:
This day was like a journey into the past. I wrapped up my business call early, about 3:30, and I found a park to run in that reminded me so much of Watertown. I have come to appreciate more than ever the natural beauty and all that goes with it outdoors; the smell of grass, for instance. I ran two miles as fast as I could. To run close to the limit is my definition of life, the total mastery of movement. I can remember that feeling on those autumn evenings in high school, of running and then coming home and eating Mom's supper and thinking that it tasted better than anything I'd ever eaten before. Those images will stay with me forever, I guess. It's like that when I think about us, the good thoughts. Both of us seem to be singularly favored. It's like we found a fortune when we met, a new type of wealth for both of us. We have grown rapidly, probably because we are both winning every day in every thing we try. It's the only way to live.

Love,
Steve

They felt comfortable together, Connie and Steve. Their backgrounds and families were similar. His passion to will himself into a whole person once again moved her. "You're coming back," she reminded him often. "You can do it. Whatever the goal, if it satisfies a person's feeling of purpose, it will create happiness and happiness is what everyone deserves. I want that for you, Steve. For both of us."

Like Steve, Connie had set her standards high, and when she didn't reach them she brooded, withdrawing into herself. At those times Steve would sense her need for support and he would comfort her, his arms wrapped around her, his eyes holding hers and giving her purpose.

Although she had already begun to run before she met Steve, she had never before known a runner of his intensity, and he impelled her to do more than she had ever thought possible. "It was unbelievable," she says. "He taught me about control of my mind and within weeks I was running five miles. The races thrill me—the excitement, the aura of running, the feel of running. Races are a social happening. Runners, like actors or musicians, are performers. They must deal with the same obstacles other performers deal with: self-discipline, control of body, and control of mind."

She even acquired his venial sin of trying to get too far too fast. She ran 100 miles in two weeks and her body rebelled with aches in muscles she never knew she had. "I learned what serious runners face all the time," she says. "That you must know your own limit and respect it."

Connie always was a doer, accepting nothing less than her maximum effort. And, like Steve, a dreamer. "Steve is a great dreamer, just like me—maybe more so," she told a friend once. "He dreams of himself running in the Olympics. I've never met anyone who sets his goals so high and who has so much determination to realize his dream, to feel it and taste it. I mean, he can *see* himself running in the Games."

His deep reserve of strength could not help but naturally influence her. Playing a game in a racquetball tournament and losing 11–20, Steve, a spectator, coached her, imploring her to concentrate on her serves and take her time. She did, staging a furious rally that brought her a 21–20 win. As they walked back to her apartment later, Steve outlined for her a three-step program on how to become a women's Class A racquetball player. Connie nodded and beamed at him; she tingled with the exhilaration she felt in winning. And her capacity to come back had made Steve proud of her. She was solid steel, he thought.

It fit their dual philosophy of helping each other achieve. Happiness. Growth. Winning every day.

Days were spent together. And they grew closer. Steve had bought an engagement ring and while engagement had been discussed often, there had never been the right moment to finalize it.

That October Sunday was soft and cool and Bloomington was lovely. The weather was clear and the trees were beginning to deepen in hue. They walked. He took her hand, slipping his fingers between hers. He had intended to ask her to marry him but that wasn't how it happened. Both of them began talking at once of wedding ideas, of a life together, of hopes and dreams. She put a finger to his lips and shushed him. Standing on her tiptoes, she slid her hands around his neck and kissed him. He leaned down and kissed her hair. She was supremely happy, happier than she could remember ever being. Steve was overwhelmed by the moment, placing the ring on her finger, and he knew a joy that some people never even approach.

Southern Indiana in the deepest months of autumn is a thing of beauty. The hills and knobs that lie between the Wabash and Ohio rivers, undisturbed by the glaciers of centuries ago, are blanketed with thick stands of maple, birch, ash, elm, and sycamore trees that glimmer in the autumn glade of reds and yellows and browns and oranges.

Each day has its own color and shape. Each day has its own hour that is special, a time that atones for all others, so tranquil that it seems to let a runner fly in a space all his own.

For Steve, that hour is in the early morning, after the sun has established itself. It was on such a day, a golden prelude to Indian summer, that he slathered Vaseline on his feet and then began, under a pure sky that was the palest of blues, running on a lonely road that led him to a wooden bridge.

The slap! slap! of his footfall on the rutted boards was distinct. The bridge took him across a wide reservoir, from which a morning mist seemed to be suspended like smoke above the water. This was a run that he made often, for at no other time did he feel so airy, so free, so immersed. It was a retreat, a place to steal away and eliminate the worries from the mind.

Soon after he left the bridge, his steps carried him into a different world, one of sycamores and oaks and maples, splashed with color, and consuming him in a forest of rich odors of grass and leaves that drenched his senses.

Somewhere, there was the muffled barking of dogs and then silence settled in once more. He was aware of his heavy breathing and the sun that peeked through the opening in the trees as he ran. He turned left. The road took him into the country. He was alone and with the feeling in his body of every step he was taking. Lord, the serenity he felt. It was a tonic, a rush that surged through his veins.

Overhead a jet streaked, trailed by a fuzzy white serpentine tail. He shut his eyes and threw his head back. Swiftly—neatly —he was for one moment perfect again, all the things he wanted to be at once. Ahead an old white, wooden church loomed. The church was surrounded by a wall of stone, pieces that had been loosely put into place.

He was now into the fourteenth mile of his run. He swung onto a gravel road and freewheeled down a hill, his hair floating behind him. A small stream crossed the road in front of him but he did not stop. He stepped into the ankle-deep water and with four steps traversed the stream.

The road rose sharply. Water squishing in his shoes, he pulled hard with his arms. Climbing. Climbing. Climbing. Breathing deeply, he hit the top of the rise and then he was able to settle into a steady rhythm on a long, flat stretch of road flanked on either side by open fields and a few trees. Over him was the big sky and the whisper of wind voices.

It was on this run that he often let his mind slip into a fantasy, placing himself at the starting line for the 5,000-meter run at the 1980 National AAU meet. Squeezing his eyes shut, it all became crystal clear . . . Lost in his daydream he can hear the sound of the starter's gun, he can *feel* the mass of arms and legs all pushing off together, he can sense the quickening of the pace and inwardly a voice is shouting:

". . . Moscow! Da! . . .

". . . Moscow! Da!"

The AAU meet will precede the 1980 Olympic Trials. It will determine who the favorites are for the three available places in the 5,000 on the American team that will go to Moscow.

. . . A form without weight, running in a snowfall at night, the whitecaps on Lake Kampeska, rain in Kiev, a car out of control, a body in the street, a deathless vortex of space, the tears, a dark sun, a return, a return, a return, a return . . .

Heidi snapped back to reality. As he ran he was awash with

a great dose of Indiana sunshine on his shoulder blades. His developed thighs, flat belly, narrow hips, tendons, bones, muscles, all were firmly articulated—all moved as one. His body glistened with perspiration.

As far as the eye could see stretched the fields and trees and the rolling road in front of him. Flaxen grass in the field rippled in a puff of wind.

There is contentment that comes from a deep breath of fresh country air. He breathed deeply, feeling his heart pounding evenly as he ran. Peace. He was at peace with himself.

He was alive. He was running.